THE FOUR
FUNDAMENTALS OF
SMOKING

THE FOUR FUNDAMENTALS OF
SMOKING

Pit Master Secrets to Making
Incredible BBQ at Home

CHRIS SUSSMAN
Founder of The BBQ Buddha

PAGE STREET
PUBLISHING CO.

PAGE STREET
PUBLISHING CO.

First published in 2021 by

Page Street Publishing Co.

27 Congress Street, Suite 105

Salem, MA 01970

www.pagestreetpublishing.com

Distributed by Macmillan, sales in Canada by The Canadian Manda Group.

25 24 23 22 21   1 2 3 4 5

ISBN-13: 978-1-64567-241-8

ISBN-10: 1-64567-241-7

Library of Congress Control Number: 2020944182

Cover and book design by Laura Benton for Page Street Publishing Co.

Photography by Chris Sussman

Food styling by Sara Rounsavall

Printed and bound in the United States of America

I'D LIKE TO DEDICATE THIS BOOK TO MY WIFE, DEBBIE SUSSMAN, A.K.A. "MRS. BUDDHA." THERE'S NO ONE I'D RATHER BE SHARING THIS JOURNEY WITH. HERE'S TO "SLIDING IN SIDEWAYS"!

PART 2: THE RECIPES ⋆ 65

THINGS THAT GO "CLUCK" (. . . AND "GOBBLE") ✶ 123

INTRODUCTION

Do you find yourself struggling to make a brisket worthy of praise from friends and family? Have you been frustrated with your pulled pork not being tender enough to actually pull? Do your smoked ribs come out dry and chewy? Or do you feel like your BBQ is pretty good, but not as good as it could be? If you answered yes to any of these questions, then this book is for you!

I, too, struggled with all of these issues for years until I finally realized there are certain fundamentals to smoking and backyard BBQ that must be mastered in order to produce the results you are hoping for. When I started getting feedback from people who attended my classes that the fundamentals they learned from me changed their personal BBQ journey, I knew I was onto something. It has been years in the making, but now I have distilled my experience into four basic yet important fundamentals and am excited to share them with you in this book!

In the following pages, you will learn the Four Fundamentals of Smoking, which will empower you to master the art of backyard BBQ. Fundamental 1 is where I will introduce the different types of fuel, combustion and wood to use. Fundamental 2 is where you will learn the importance of controlling humidity and its impact on your BBQ. Fundamental 3 is all about controlling temperature and the ins and outs of the "BBQ Zone." Finally, Fundamental 4 is where I share my secrets of knowing how to tell when your BBQ is done.

After we go over the fundamentals, I will introduce you to some of my favorite recipes and techniques, putting together the fundamentals into practice with real-life examples. But how did I get here? What did I do to learn these tips and tricks to share with you?

MY STORY

Everyone's BBQ story is a journey, and all journeys have to start somewhere, so let me take you to where mine all began . . .

When I was a young child, around 6 years old, my family often drove down to Norfolk, Virginia, to visit my grandparents. As we were driving down the last stretch of Interstate 64, my dad would stop at Pierce's Pitt Bar-B-Que in Williamsburg, Virginia. I'll never forget his order, as he would always order the same thing: a pulled pork sandwich topped with creamy coleslaw and an ice-cold Dr Pepper, in one of those classic "hobble skirt" bottles, on the side. Sitting there sharing that experience with my dad forever imprinted on me that deep smokey flavor of the pulled pork paired with the cool, tangy sweetness of the slaw. That's when my love for BBQ truly began.

Fast-forward to 2009 and the role was reversed; I was now a father and had two children of my own. At that time, I was cooking on a gas grill—until my wife got me Steven Raichlen's book *BBQ USA*, and everything changed on my BBQ journey. I got my first smoker, a Weber Smokey Mountain, and started learning the craft of BBQ one cook at a time, slowly but surely fueling my passion and desire to make great BBQ. From spatchcock chicken to whole packer brisket, I was committed to honing the craft.

Continuing on this newfound passion, the next big moment in my BBQ journey came a few years later when I got my first Big Green Egg. My love for cooking BBQ, specifically smoking meat, kicked into high gear. This grill design allowed me to cook year-round and, living in a state that has all four seasons, I took advantage of that. This grill introduced me to a whole new group of people known as "EGG Heads" and to branded festivals known as "EGG Fests." In 2015, I cooked with the Dizzy Pig competition BBQ team at several festivals including EGGtoberfest, hosted by Big Green Egg in Atlanta. During the next several years, I competed with the EGGcellent Eats cook team that took runner-up twice in the People's Choice competition, finally winning in 2017, a great and well-deserved accomplishment I was proud to be a part of.

Since then, my recipes and associated videos have been featured on the Big Green Egg website, I have joined the Big Green Egg Pro Staff, secured sponsorships with some of my favorite brands and now travel around the country doing classes and demos. Up until 2018, it's hard to believe I was pursuing my BBQ passions and still working a corporate job in the IT field. Once I realized that I could share my love and teaching of BBQ with others, I left my corporate job of more than twenty years to pursue this path full time. That's where my nickname comes in: "The BBQ Buddha." My goal is to take you on this journey to BBQ Nirvana with me.

Now that I have you all on this journey with me, I cook with a 250-gallon offset smoker named Esther, a Traeger Pellet Grill, that old Weber Smokey Mountain I started on and more Big Green Eggs than I can count. I spend every day creating new recipes for my many social media channels and connecting with people just like you, to help and encourage their own BBQ journeys. As you read through this cookbook, I think it'll be clear that this is my passion and my life.

I can only hope that this book will do for you what *BBQ USA* did for me many years ago and ignites your passion for BBQ and smoking meats!

PART 1

THE FOUR FUNDAMENTALS OF SMOKING

FUEL, COMBUSTION AND WOOD

How to Build a Fire for Optimal BBQ Smoke

You have heard that old saying "when there's smoke there's fire," but is that a true statement? Have you thought about that phrase in context to your own BBQ experience? What kind of fire produces smoke? Which smoke is the best for BBQ? Well, one of my first "aha" moments in my own personal BBQ journey was realizing that the way I thought about smoke was not necessarily how smoke flavor is imparted to food. To start honing my BBQ skills, I had to take a step back and think about where that smoke flavor comes from and how to manage the fire that creates it.

Let me introduce some important concepts for you to start: fuel source, combustion and wood. I'll explain each at a high level then dive deeper as we continue through this chapter.

FUEL SOURCE	The way in which your grill creates heat and maintains that heat for the duration of your cook. Some common fuel sources are gas, electricity and charcoal.
COMBUSTION	How you will start the fire using your fuel source of choice. Some common fire starters are fire starter cubes, hand torches and electric lighters.
WOOD	Comes in the form of hardwoods, softwoods, nutwoods and fruitwoods that release certain chemicals in the form of a vapor that both color and flavor the BBQ. Some common woods are hickory, apple, oak and pecan.

The type of grill you have at home will impact the way in which you think about managing the fire. I have a Traeger Timberline (pellet grill) and it does all of the work for me. The only action you need to take in order to manage temperature on this grill is accessing the app on your smartphone, as this type of grill controls everything else. If you own this type of grill, just pick the wood pellets you want to use, make sure you have enough in the hopper for the duration of the cook and press a button. These grills put out excellent BBQ and the ease of use makes them a smart choice for many people. With the two other grills I own—a Big Green Egg (kamado grill) and a Weber Smokey Mountain (bullet grill)—I need to consider which fuel type to use (heat source), how to light it (combustion) and where I will get the smoke color and flavor from (wood type).

So, what is smoke? What is in it that creates the familiar BBQ flavor we are looking for? Well, smoke is a combination of steam from the water burning off in the wood, tiny particles mixed in with the vapor and (most important) gases that do 90 percent of the work flavoring and coloring your food. If you are grilling at home, you are most likely using fuel in the form of charcoal, gas or electricity as the way to start and maintain the fire in your grill. In order for you to get at the gases necessary for the smoke flavor, you also need wood in the form of pellets, chunks or chips. Inside the wood is a compound called *lignin*, making up to a third of the wood's composition. When wood is burned at a certain temperature (570°F [299°C]) it breaks down to a series of chemicals called *phenols* and *carbonyls*. Those chemicals create the smokey flavor and dark color you are looking for.

For charcoal grill owners, the first step is picking the right fuel for your fire. You want to find something that lights fast, burns clean and lasts long enough for your cook time. Your choices are lump charcoal, charcoal briquettes or logs of wood. Let's look at each and figure out which is best for you and your grill.

LUMP CHARCOAL	Created by burning wood without oxygen, leaving behind charcoaled chunks of wood. Some lump charcoal includes fillers or additives; look for those that do not. Lump charcoal burns hotter and faster than its briquette counterpart and is my preferred fuel source. My preferred brands are Fogo and Big Green Egg.
CHARCOAL BRIQUETTES	Made up of a mix of sawdust and leftover wood material. Most are processed with fillers and chemicals to hold the briquettes together. They last longer but do not burn as hot as lump charcoal; therefore, they are not my favorite fuel source.
WOOD LOGS	Cut from trees and comes in various forms, from green to kiln-dried, neither of which can be used in smoking. The type of smokers we're covering in this book don't take whole wood logs as a fuel source at all. Only a specialized offset smoker can use real wood logs; therefore this is not a preferred fuel source for our purposes.

Fogo is my favorite brand of lump charcoal to use (back left). Other options for fuel are briquettes (back right) and wood logs (front).

A sample of wood chips (upper) and wood chunks (lower). Each work well, but for different reasons—use chips for short cooks and chunks for longer cooks.

I strongly recommend using lump charcoal as a fuel source. This type of fuel burns hot and gets you the temperatures needed to release the phenols from the lignin in the wood. In addition, you do not get any unwanted flavors released into your food as it is made without fillers and chemicals. There are several brands on the market that make good lump charcoal. My favorite by far is Fogo Charcoal.

If you choose to use charcoal as your primary fuel source, you'll need to supplement it with a wood product to get a smokey flavor. For kamado and charcoal grills, such as the Big Green Egg and Weber Smokey Mountain Cooker, use either wood chunks or wood chips. Wood chunks and chips come in every different wood type that is popular for traditional BBQ. The difference between chunks and

chips is size. Chunks are fist-sized pieces of wood and chips come as pieces about the size of a quarter.

When would you use wood chips versus wood chunks? Wood chips are made up of scrap wood pieces and shavings. They burn quickly and are primarily used for quick bursts of smoke flavor for shorter cooking times (e.g., steaks, fish or smaller cuts of pork or chicken). Wood chunks take longer to ignite and burn for an extended period of time, making them ideal for low and slow BBQ cooking. The best way to use either is to mix them with your lump charcoal before lighting the grill. In each recipe in this book, I will suggest which size (chunks versus chips) as well as which variety of wood (oak, pecan, apple, etc.) that I recommend for that particular recipe.

WOOD	WOOD TYPE	FLAVOR	NOTES
Alder	Forest	Medium	Great with seafood
Apple	Orchard	Medium	Easiest to use out of the orchard woods
Cherry	Orchard	Medium	A good wood to blend with other wood types because cherry imparts a distinct yellow color, as well as a mild flavor profile
Hickory	Forest	Full	Most common BBQ wood used
Pecan	Forest	Full	Has a unique, sweet flavor profile that is great with beef and chicken
Oak	Forest	Bold	This is what Texas BBQ is all about
Mesquite	Forest	Very bold	Should be used sparingly

Let's take a look at the various wood types you can use for smoking shown in the table above. In addition, I will add suggested wood types to each recipe, giving you help to make these choices when cooking on your own. I will keep my focus on the most common wood types found at the places that sell BBQ supplies. However, keep in mind that there are lots of other options out there that you can explore when you start to really master the foundations.

Now that we have introduced the type of fuel (lump charcoal) and wood (chips or chunks) for BBQ, let's discuss lighting the fire and the temperature needed to break down the wood and to release those important, yet volatile chemicals known as phenols.

As discussed at the beginning of this chapter, the smoke that you see when you first light your fire isn't the stuff that imparts those flavors into your food. In fact, that white billowy "smoke" is actually mostly steam from the moisture inside the wood, other acidic gases and creosote that will leave an acrid flavor in your food.

What you are looking for is the sweet spot when wood burns hot enough to release both carbonyls, which give BBQ that distinctive mahogany color, and phenols, which give BBQ its smokey taste. This temperature is around 700°F (371°C), which simultaneously breaks down the lignin and is hot enough to burn off the unwanted vapors and particles that leave an unpleasant taste on food.

FIRE STARTER CUBES	Small wood cubes that are odorless and tasteless from brands such as SpeediLight. Place two or three of these buried about halfway in with the lump charcoal and light with a match or butane lighter.
BUTANE HAND TORCH	Using a tank of butane gas, this handheld torch lights the lump charcoal fast. Popular brands include Bernzomatic.
LOOFTLIGHTER	This tool uses super-heated air to start a fire in 60 seconds.

Please note that 700°F (371°C) is not the temperature of your grill, but rather the temperature of the wood combustion happening inside the cooker. Lucky for you the way to know if the wood has reached this temperature is easy: just watch the smoke billowing from your smoker. Once it turns from cloudy white to blueish gray, your smoke is running clean and you have the right environment in place for the best BBQ. The key to getting your fuel source to burn hot enough is oxygen from controlling the airflow of your charcoal smokers.

As for lighting the fuel source (combustion), you have several options to choose from. Let's take a look at the three most popular above.

Each of the methods for lighting the fire has their place, and I use them interchangeably. However, for the beginner I think it is best to start with fire starter cubes. You can add two or three pieces to the lump charcoal, light them, walk away and come back in 10 minutes to a nice fire ready for you to manage.

You will learn all the details of how to build, light and maintain your fire in Fundamental 3: Controlling Temperature and the BBQ Zone.

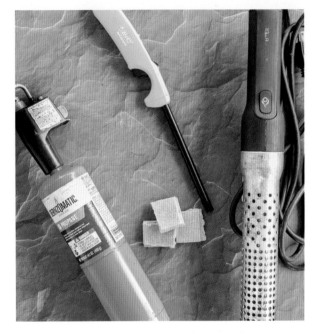

There are lots of options for fire starters, including a common lighter, fire starter cubes, a butane hand torch (left) and a LooftLighter (right). Fire starter cubes are the best for beginners.

CONTROLLING HUMIDITY

How to Capture Smoke Flavor in Your Meat

As I wrote in Fundamental 1: Fuel, Combustion and Wood, smoke is more than just what you see. In fact, smoke is a mixture of oils, liquid droplets and vapors. The oils and liquid present themselves in the form of white or black smoke. This "smoke" is actually tiny compounds and particles contained in the steam released by the moisture in wood as it burns. When oil and liquid fall onto the meat, which is full of water, they run off the surface and are not absorbed. Vapors, on the other hand, are gases that your eyes cannot see. These vapors are what do most of the work to create flavor and to color meat.

So what is absorbed and how? The chemicals that are released in the vapors will stick to the surface of your meat if it is slightly wet and tacky. As the chemicals in the vapors fall onto that surface, they work their way into the center of the food, creating changes to both color and flavor. The trick to BBQ, and to using your grill, is to manage that slightly wet surface so it can fully absorb the vapor compounds being released by the burning wood.

The area of focus for you as the meat is smoking is to ensure the formation of the pellicle. The pellicle is a very thin layer that forms on the surface of the meat as its proteins break down and form polymers. This layer, when managed properly, is the key to getting the gases absorbed into the meat for both coloring and flavoring. A well-formed pellicle comes from the carbonyls and phenols in the vapor. Their interaction with the proteins, sugars and starches on the food's surface creates this important layer.

It is worth noting that bark formation is the end result of this exercise. What you want is for your meat to have a deep mahogany color and a hard crust-like substance on the outside of the meat. To get that end result you must focus on managing the pellicle as the meat is slowly cooking inside. To form the pellicle, you need the humidity in your grill to be between 70 and 80 percent. As you monitor the meat while it's smoking, the balancing act is to form a pellicle that is slightly wet and feels gummy, without getting it too wet or too dry. If the surface is too wet, the dry rub will run off, taking with it the gases that should be absorbed into the meat, and the bark formation will be streaky. Conversely, you do not want the surface too dry, as the moisture needed to absorb the gases isn't there, which results in little to no smoke flavor or coloration.

There are various techniques to manage humidity in your smoker. I will introduce them here and we will explore each in more detail as the chapter progresses.

The first factor to consider is the insulation of your smoker. If the inside environment is impacted too much by the outside environment, it will be harder to maintain the necessary humidity. A simple pan of water is a great way to add humidity to the smoker. Use an aluminum pan full of warm water placed in the smoker (if needed) to help maintain that humidity level during a long cook. Alternatively, misting the BBQ with a spray bottle of water can help manage the humidity level. Last, mopping (a technique using a small mop or brush to impart moisture and aromatics onto the meat) is a great way to manage the moisture level on the surface of the meat and to layer in flavor at the same time.

Let's break down each technique, looking at the details to think through when planning your cook.

INSULATED ENVIRONMENT AND THE NEED FOR A WATER PAN

A Traeger Timberline is a well-insulated grill and is not impacted by the outside environment. In addition, this grill uses convection cooking, which circulates the air in a way that keeps the cooking environment moist. The natural moisture in the environment comes from the steam released from the wood pellets burning inside, as well as from the moisture in the meat cooking off and evaporating. However, while the Traeger handles the humidity for you, you still need to manage the pellicle formation. The best way to do so is by using a spritz or a mop, which I'll elaborate on later in this chapter.

The Big Green Egg has the most insulation of the grills discussed in this book, as this grill is made entirely out of ceramic, an exceptional insulator. In addition, the egg-shaped design creates a natural convection that helps to circulate moisture while the meat is cooking. Again, as this grill is well insulated, moisture is introduced from the charcoal as well as from the wood burning and creating steam. The meat also releases moisture as it cooks down, releasing its internal water content. Because of the design of this grill, you do not need to add a water pan during the cook. You do, however, need to use a spritz or a mop at a certain point in the cook to manage pellicle formation. We will go into this in just a bit.

SPRAY RECIPES

PORK

1 cup (240 ml) apple juice

1 cup (240 ml) apple cider vinegar

Several dashes ($\frac{1}{4}$–$\frac{1}{2}$ tsp) each of Worcestershire sauce and hot sauce, to taste

BEEF

1 cup (240 ml) apple cider vinegar

1 cup (240 ml) water

Several dashes ($\frac{1}{4}$–$\frac{1}{2}$ tsp) each of Worcestershire sauce and hot sauce, to taste

The Weber Smokey Mountain is not well insulated compared with the other two grills mentioned and, as a result, is impacted by external factors such as wind and cold. In addition, the design of this bullet smoker uses a water pan to create the indirect cooking zone needed for low and slow BBQ. With this style of grill, the water pan is an essential part of not only managing the humidity, but also creating the cooking environment needed to produce great BBQ. For this type of smoker, as you're already using a water pan, there is a lot of moisture in the environment to help with pellicle formation. You'll therefore be less dependent on spritzing and mopping than with the other smokers.

SPRAY BOTTLES AND MOPS

As we just covered, spray bottles and mops are critical components when cooking on the Traeger or Big Green Egg cookers. When you're cooking on the Weber Smokey Mountain, mopping and spritzing aren't as important because the cooker already includes a water pan that increases the humidity needed for proper pellicle formation.

When tending to a long cook, it is your job to watch the meat as it changes in color, size and shape. As you monitor the progress, it is important to focus on the moisture level on the outside of the meat as explained above. Even with a well-insulated grill or the use of a water pan, the surface of the meat may begin to dry out. To manage this, use a spray bottle or a mop to add moisture to the surface.

When using either method, it is important to wait to begin spraying or mopping until the meat has been smoking for 3 uninterrupted hours for larger cuts of meat, e.g., brisket and pork shoulder. For smaller cuts like pork ribs, begin to spray or mop after the first hour. The first 1 to 3 hours of any BBQ cook is critical to setting the bark and forming the pellicle.

SPRAY BOTTLES: With a spray bottle, you are looking to mist moisture on the meat's surface area. Be careful to mist lightly and not add so much liquid that the meat becomes too wet that the dry rub runs off. Use a good-quality sprayer that mists evenly; avoid the type of bottle that sends out streams of water. It's not necessary to use anything other than water because the flavor you are looking to highlight comes from the meat and smoke. However, some people like to use other liquids in their spray bottle to help layer flavors during the long cook. Some common flavors for various cooks are listed in the box above.

MOP RECIPES

PORK

1 cup (240 ml) apple cider vinegar

½ cup (120 ml) water

1 tsp kosher salt

1 tsp black pepper

1 tsp paprika

1 tsp dry mustard

1 tsp hot sauce

1 tsp garlic powder

BEEF

1 cup (240 ml) beef stock

½ cup (120 ml) water

½ cup (120 ml) Worcestershire sauce

2 tbsp (30 ml) canola oil

2 cloves garlic, minced

1 tbsp (5 g) red pepper flakes

1 tsp kosher salt

1 tsp black pepper

1 tsp paprika

1 tsp onion powder

MOPS: This is a way to add moisture to the surface area of the meat by spreading liquid on it as it cooks during a long smoking session. It is called "mopping" because you are using a miniature mop to apply liquid to the surface area. Mops are available in any BBQ store or online. Alternatively, you can use a basting brush, but the mop head is softer and has less impact on bark formation. When using a basting brush, you run the risk of wiping off the spices that form the bark.

When using the mop method, you are layering flavor into the bark in addition to managing moisture and pellicle formation. When using a mop, be careful not to disturb the bark before it sets or to leave too much moisture on the surface. Remember to watch the pellicle formation carefully, as that will tell you where you need to mop (i.e., where the dry spots on the surface of the meat are). My favorite mop recipes are listed in the box to the left.

Now that we have covered these important concepts, let's put it together so you know when and where to take action during your long cook. The concept is the same for every recipe you smoke, but the variables change depending on the cut of meat you are working with. I will outline the process for common meats on page 27.

The most important thing to watch for is to see where wet or dry spots are forming. Manage wet spots as they appear by tilting the meat to let moisture build up and run off. As dry spots appear, use the spritzing/mopping techniques described earlier. Do not be afraid to move your meat around the smoker, as one side may be getting more heat than the other. Because there is no way to measure the humidity level of your grill, using your senses of sight and touch are critical to this phase of the cook; you have to continually watch the meat to monitor the humidity level. We will go into more detail on pellicle, bark and color formation in Fundamental 4: The Finish (page 41).

For the most common cuts, here's the timing and work flow to manage humidity and pellicle formation.

BRISKET AND PORK SHOULDER

First 3 hours: Let it cook; don't do anything!

At hour four, start checking the pellicle (i.e., the surface of the meat). What you are looking for is a dark color forming and for the surface to be sticky. If you see and feel this, that's great. However, if you see moisture building up in a certain spot on the surface of your BBQ, lift and tilt the meat cooking inside to allow it to run off. If the surface is dry, spritz or mop it to add moisture to the surface and cooking environment. Continue doing this every hour until the bark is formed (this usually takes 6 hours).

RIBS

After the first hour, start checking the pellicle. If it's wet and streaky, don't do anything. If it's dry, spritz or mop it. Continue doing this every 30 minutes until the bark is formed (this usually takes 3 to 4 hours).

CHICKEN

After the first 30 minutes, start checking the pellicle. If it's wet and streaky, don't do anything. If it's dry, spritz or mop it. Continue doing this every 30 minutes as needed until the bark is formed (this usually takes 3 to 4 hours).

CONTROLLING TEMPERATURE AND THE BBQ ZONE

The Secrets to Managing Your Fire for Traditional BBQ

We have reviewed controlling airflow to your grill to manage combustion and, in turn, the smoke that the wood produces for color and flavor. In addition, we have covered how to think about and control the needed humidity in your grill to lay the foundation to which all that wonderful smoke flavor can adhere. Now, let's discuss the internal temperature of your grill, why it is key to successful smoking and, most importantly, why it needs to be between 225 and 275°F (107 and 135°C) to make the BBQ magic happen.

First, let's clarify the differences between grilling and BBQ, which many people get mixed up about. These are key factors to know when getting into the BBQ game. Think of grilling as the ability to cook smaller cuts of meat like steaks, chicken breasts or pork chops directly over live fire in a short period of time. You can still infuse a bit of smoke to this type of cooking by using wood chips (see page 17 in Fundamental 1: Fuel, Combustion and Wood). A lot of people talk about coming over for a BBQ when in fact they mean grilling hamburgers and hot dogs.

When you are cooking true BBQ, it has to be low and slow, which allows you to break down the fat and collagen in larger cuts of meat (e.g., pork shoulder, brisket, pork spareribs) while taking on the color and flavor of the smoke in which the meat is cooking. At the end of the day, you may be using the same grill to cook your hamburgers as you do to smoke your brisket, but those burgers are not true BBQ.

	GRILLING (HOT AND FAST)	BBQ (LOW AND SLOW)
COOKING METHOD	Direct: Food is cooked directly over the heat source	Indirect: The food is offset from the heat source or has a heat shield/baffle to create an indirect cooking environment
COOKING TEMPERATURE	350–500°F (176–260°C)	225–275°F (107–135°C)
COOKING TIME	Less than 1 hour	8–16 hours

	BEEF	PORK	CHICKEN
USDA RECOMMENDED	145°F (63°C)	145°F (63°C)	165°F (74°C)
RARE	120–130°F (49–54°C)	N/A	N/A
MEDIUM-RARE	125–135°F (52–57°C)	N/A	N/A
MEDIUM	135–145°F (57–63°C)	135–145°F (57–63°C)	N/A
MEDIUM-WELL	145–155°F (63–68°C)	145–155°F (63–68°C)	N/A
WELL-DONE	155–160°F (68–71°C)	150–160°F (66–71°C)	N/A

There are three major differences between grilling and BBQ: method, temperature and time, which you can review in the table above.

As I stated earlier, not everything you make on your cooker is BBQ. There are several additional factors that go into explaining the difference between these two cooking methods and several variables you need to manage to produce great BBQ, no matter which method you're using. The general concepts of these factors are listed briefly below, and then on the next pages we will unpack each factor in more depth.

FOOD TEMPERATURES: Understanding the difference between the USDA recommended temperature and the actual finished temperature helps create great BBQ and grilled meats.

DENATURING: The proteins in meat react differently at different temperatures, which explains why a lower temperature helps produce the best-tasting BBQ.

TIMING AND SIZE: A lower temperature lengthens the time of your cook, so you need to understand the variables that can change that equation. The size of the meat will dictate the denaturing process and the timing of your cook.

CARRYOVER COOKING AND RESTING: Resting is one of the most important factors to great BBQ and carryover cooking is the reason why.

FACTOR 1—FOOD TEMPERATURES

Let's review food safety temperatures for the most common BBQ meats: beef, pork and chicken.

The chart on the previous page covers what the USDA says is the safe temperature for when these types of meat are done. To use this guide, you cook your meat to the internal temperature listed above and it will be safe to serve. However, the USDA temps do not tell the whole story, and they are just a reference point when cooking BBQ. Let's explore what happens to meat when it is cooking (i.e., how heat affects the composition of meat as it cooks).

FACTOR 2—DENATURING

Meat is composed of several muscle fibers that are intertwined in a way that creates long protein strands. When cooked, these protein strands shrink, brown and lose moisture, known as denaturing. Denaturing is, in essence, changing the structure of the proteins.

Why is this important? Well, at certain internal temperatures specific proteins are affected in different ways. The two most important are myosin and actin. Myosin is the thicker of the two. As it denatures, it impacts the texture and look of the meat, causing it to go from raw to cooked. The key internal temperature affecting myosin is 122°F (50°C), which is when the meat is cooked but it has still retained most of its moisture (e.g., medium-rare steak).

Actin is the thinner of the two proteins and denatures at the much higher internal temperature of 150°F (66°C). If you reach an internal temperature in your meat that causes the actin to denature, this will result in too much moisture loss and contraction, which leaves you with dry and tough meat (e.g., a medium-well or well-done steak).

The trick to cooking is to find that sweet spot when myosin denatures, but actin does not. You may be asking yourself, "Since most BBQ is cooked to a final temperature between 190°F (88°C) and 204°F (65°C), how can you produce juicy and moist BBQ if the actin has denatured?" To help answer that, let's take a look at the next factor: timing and size.

FACTOR 3—TIMING AND SIZE

Cooking meat is a simple formula: time multiplied by temperature (i.e., the higher the temperature, the shorter amount of time is needed to cook the meat). The two variables are relative to one another and that is an important concept to keep in mind.

The way in which you should think about timing is this: Smaller and thinner cuts should get higher heat and shorter cook times. The larger cuts should have lower heat and longer cook times. In low and slow BBQ the meat will always reach the temperature at which actin is denatured, which normally would make for tough and dry meat. However, because the cooking temperature has been kept relatively low, the slow rendering of collagen releases additional moisture in the form of gelatin, which makes up for the moisture lost from the actin. This lubricant is rich and gelatinous, and it encases the meat fibers, giving them a rich and decadent flavor and mouthfeel.

It is important to note that the temperature of your smoker isn't hot enough to boil off the moisture released from the muscle fibers or the gelatin created from the rendered collagen. But why? What is it about cooking larger cuts of meat that causes this? Let us dive into the second part of Factor 3: size.

Here I will introduce you to the concept of temperature gradient. To understand this, you need to understand that the way heat moves through meat is not linear. The meat you are barbecuing absorbs the heat from your grill as energy. Energy works its way into the meat, and as it moves toward the center, the energy reduces. This means the outer layers retain higher temperatures compared to the inner layers. The more energy released in the cooking environment (i.e., the higher the temperature of your grill), the more energy is imparted to your meat. In large, thick cuts of meat, a lot of energy again means the outer layers will overcook before the energy reaches the middle.

For tender, moist barbecued meats, you want the inner layers to cook at the same rate as the outer layers—and to do this, lower heat and a longer amount of time are needed. In this way, the temperature gradient is managed and evened out, allowing the larger cuts of meat to cook evenly.

But there is one more element involved: how the temperature affects the meat after it is done. Why is that important? Let's look at Factor 4 to find out.

FACTOR 4—CARRYOVER COOKING AND RESTING

As discussed in Factor 3, as energy makes its way from the grill to the outside of the meat to the center of the meat, the outside layers of the meat retain more energy than the inner layers. So, what happens when you pull meat off the grill? Well, it continues cooking until that energy in the outer layers starts to dissipate. The larger the cut, the more carryover cooking there will be. You can expect the internal temperature of your meat to be anywhere from five to ten degrees higher after you pull it off the grill because of carryover cooking.

This factor is much more important with smaller cuts of grilled meat than it is in traditional BBQ. This is the reason you should always grill meat five to ten degrees less than your desired end temperature. The carryover cooking will bring the meat to your desired temperature, ensuring a delicious end result. With traditional BBQ, temperature isn't the only factor to consider in determining when your BBQ is done, as you'll read in Fundamental 4: The Finish, so carryover cooking isn't as important as resting.

Resting is arguably the most important factor to serving great BBQ. When you rest your meat, it allows the backyard pit master to be in control of serving the best possible end product to the guests when they arrive. Resting larger cuts of meat such as brisket and pork shoulder allows the moisture and collagen produced during the cook to be reabsorbed into the meat. This step is probably the most overlooked by home cooks when they are first learning BBQ. When you pull one of these large cuts of meat from the smoker, you should always rest it at least 2 hours before slicing and serving.

To rest your BBQ at home, wrap the meat in aluminum foil (or butcher paper—more on that later) and then wrap that in an old towel. That meat should then go into a cooler (without ice of course) for 2 to 3 hours before you serve it. This is the optimal way and time to rest the BBQ that you have spent 10 to 12 hours cooking for your guests.

★ NOTE ★

Remember that water boils at 212°F (100°C). You never want the internal temperature of your meat to get close to that point on the grill (or off), as it will start boiling off moisture, resulting in dry meat.

Putting all of this together, you have a small window to play with as it pertains to the ideal BBQ temperature zone: 225 to 275°F (107 to 135°C), which I call the "BBQ Zone." This temperature range is low enough to consistently cook the outer layers of larger cuts of meat as the energy works its way to the center of the meat. But think about the type and quality of meat you are cooking (see page 42 in Fundamental 4: The Finish for more on this) before making the final decision as to the grill temperature you plan to use for your next BBQ. If you have a large and fatty cut of meat that is more forgiving (like pork shoulder), then using a higher temperature in that BBQ Zone is advisable. However, if you have a lower-grade brisket that is not well marbled, you should consider a temperature on the lower side of that scale.

CUT	SUGGESTED SMOKING TEMP
Brisket	225°F (107°C)
Pork Shoulder	275°F (135°C)
Ribs (spare & baby back)	250°F (121°C)
Ribs (beef)	225°F (107°C)
Chicken	250°F (121°C)

ENVIRONMENTAL FACTORS

Now that we have looked at some of the technical factors behind the variables of cooking BBQ, let's look at some of the environmental factors that can impact your cooking temperature: weather, humidity and altitude.

WEATHER: The first thing to consider here is whether your grill is insulated. (Note: For the cookers covered in this book, both the Traeger and the Big Green Egg are insulated.) If the grill is insulated, then the external temperature or weather will not affect your cook chamber (i.e., if it's cold outside, it won't cool down the exterior of your cooker and impact the internal temperature). However, even with an insulated smoker, cold air flowing into the fuel source will impact the internal temperature of your grill.

So, if you are cooking in colder weather, you will need to adjust for that factor by opening the Big Green Egg vents more to allow the fire to burn hotter and to offset the lower cooking chamber temp. When I am adjusting the vents on my Big Green Egg in cold weather conditions, I do so in small increments until the temperature stabilizes. It is easier to increase the temperature of this grill than decrease it. For the Traeger, you will not need to take any action, as the cooker takes care of these adjustments for you. For the Weber Smokey Mountain, you will need to think about external insulation when cooking in cold weather. You can purchase a WSM Smoker Jacket online or build something on your own. I have seen some very creative DIY instructions for this online.

HUMIDITY: The lower the humidity outside your smoker, the more that will impact the meat cooking inside. When the ambient humidity is low, your meat will express more moisture to compensate for the lack of water molecules in the air. This has the impact of cooling your meat and lengthening the time of the cook. This is the dreaded "stall" you have most likely experienced when the internal temperature of the meat stays at or near 160°F (71°C) for hours at a time.

The "Texas Crutch" is typically how you address this particular issue: wrapping your meat in foil, or what's becoming increasingly more popular, butcher paper, when you reach the stall. I will cover this in more detail in the next chapter. Another way to help with this is to think back to Fundamental 2: Controlling Humidity (page 21) and start adding that needed moisture back into the cooking environment in the form of a water pan, spray or mop.

ALTITUDE: The greater your altitude, the lower the air pressure, oxygen and humidity, which impacts your cook. For every 500 feet (152 m) above sea level, your boiling temperature drops by one degree, which doesn't affect your cooking environment too much until you hit 3,000 feet (914 m) above sea level. At that altitude, the boiling point of water has changed significantly, which in turn lowers the overall cooking temperature of your grill/smoker by as much as 10°F (5°C). In addition, the lower oxygen and humidity reduces the amount of moisture in the cooker.

To adjust for this cooking environment, you will need to increase the desired temperature of your smoker by 10°F (5°C) and add more moisture to the cook in the form of a water pan, spray or mop as covered in Fundamental 2: Controlling Humidity.

GRILL GUIDE: HOW TO SET UP AND CONTROL TEMPERATURE FOR COMMON SMOKERS

Now that we have explored the BBQ Zone and why it is important to your final product, let's take a closer look at each grill and walk through setup, lighting and managing various temperatures. What follows is a list of the grills I used for the recipes in the next section. The types of grills used for this book cover a broad spectrum of the most popular types of grills available to you. You can use the following reference material to set up and maintain the temperatures outlined for each recipe.

BIG GREEN EGG AND OTHER KAMADO-STYLE GRILLS

This grill is the one I use daily and have the most experience with. A Big Green Egg is a kamado-style cooker originally from Japan. The egg-shaped design coupled with the air vents positioned where they are creates a convection-cooking environment for superior heat distribution. The whole grill is made from ceramic and as a result is well insulated, retaining heat and protecting what's inside from the temperature outside. The fuel type for this type of grill is exclusively lump charcoal, with wood chunks or chips added for flavor. While I recommend a Big Green Egg to anyone interested in this type of cooker, there are other brands out there that offer a similar style, such as Kamado Joe and Primo Grills.

The recipes starting in the next chapter will be in two ranges: smoking (200 to 275°F [93 to 135°C]) and grilling (300 to 500°F [149 to 260°C]). I will walk you through the setup for both so you can reference each when following the recipes going forward.

Indirect Cooking: Smoking (200 to 275°F [93 to 135°C])
Load a layer of lump charcoal into the firebox, just filling the bottom a quarter of the way, then place three or four baseball-sized chunks of smoking wood on top in a triangle pattern (top, bottom right and bottom left). Fill the rest of the firebox with lump charcoal until it reaches the top of the fire ring.

Open the top and bottom vents all the way. Place a single fire starter cube toward the front of the kamado grill, buried about halfway in the lump charcoal. Light the cube and let it burn for 10 minutes.

Place the convEGGtor in the kamado grill, close the lid and leave the bottom vent and top vent wide open. Wait until the temperature rises and make sure to take action when the temperature hits 225°F (107°C) (about 20 to 30 minutes). At this point, you can make small adjustments to the bottom vent to increase the temp between 225 and 275°F (107 and 135°C).

Direct Setup: Grilling (300 to 500°F [149 to 260°C])
Fill the firebox with lump charcoal until it reaches the top of the fire ring. If you want some smoke flavor for this type of cook, add a wood chunk in with the lump charcoal using the same setup described earlier before lighting, or add a handful of wood chips after the temperature is set, right before you put the food on.

Open the top and bottom vents all the way. Place three fire starter cubes in a pyramid shape (bottom left, bottom right and top) toward the front of the kamado grill. Light the cubes and let them burn for 10 minutes.

Next, close the lid and adjust the top and bottom vents so they are 50 percent closed. Wait until the temperature rises and make sure to take action when it hits 300°F (149°C) (10 to 15 minutes). At this point, you can make small adjustments to the bottom and top vents to maintain or increase the temp between 300 and 500°F (149 and 260°C).

Indirect Cooking: Smoking (200 to 275°F [93 to 135°C])

Set up the Big Green Egg for smoking by adding a layer of charcoal and the wood chunks on top in a triangle pattern.

For smoking on the Big Green Egg, open the top vent just a little bit.

Just like the top vent, open the bottom vent only a little bit.

Direct Setup: Grilling (300 to 500°F [149 to 260°C])

For grilling on the Big Green Egg, place the fire starters in a triangle pattern.

For grilling on the Big Green Egg, open the top vent three-quarters of the way.

Just like the top vent, open the bottom vent three-quarters of the way.

WEBER SMOKEY MOUNTAIN (BULLET GRILL)

This was the very first smoker I ever purchased, enabling me to start learning the art of BBQ. This type of cooker gets its nickname from its shape, as it looks like a large bullet. The design makes it able to handle much more food than its counterpart, the kettle grill, as you have two racks to place food on. In addition, you can just open the front door to add more charcoal as you cook, without disturbing the food cooking inside. Weber says you should only use charcoal briquettes in this type of cooker, but I have used lump charcoal in mine for years without issue.

Indirect Setup: Smoking (200 to 275°F [93 to 135°C])
Start with an empty Weber Smokey Mountain and place a layer of charcoal on the bottom of the charcoal chamber, filling it about half to three-quarters full. Now add three or four baseball-sized chunks of smoking wood on top of the unlit charcoal.

Fill up a chimney starter with charcoal and light it from the bottom. Once the coals in the chimney are well lit and almost gray, dump them on top of the unlit coals and wood chunks you have loaded in the charcoal chamber.

Line the water pan with aluminum foil for easier cleanup, then add cool water to the water pan in the grill. Put the grill grates in place and put the lid on.

Leave all the vents 100 percent open while you let the cooker come up to temp, keeping a close eye on the temperature. Let the cooker get up to 250°F (121°C), then close the bottom vents all the way, leaving the top vent open.

Place your food on the grill grates. Because this cooker is not insulated, the temp will drop to about 225°F (107°C) when adding large cuts of meat. To increase or decrease the temperature, manipulate the bottom vents. I find it easier to adjust just one (as opposed to both the bottom and top vents) until the desired temperature is reached.

Set up the Weber Smokey Mountain for smoking by adding a layer of charcoal and the wood chunks on top in a triangle pattern.

Dump a chimney starter full of lit coals into the chamber.

My Traeger Timberline 1300

Direct Setup: Grilling (300 to 500°F [149 to 260°C])
Start with an empty charcoal chamber and fill a charcoal chimney two-thirds of the way with charcoal. Light the charcoal from the bottom and let the coals burn for 10 to 15 minutes, until you see the charcoal on top turn a bit gray with ash. Pour the lit charcoal into the charcoal chamber and add one chunk of wood or a handful of wood chips for smoke flavor.

Remove the water pan from your Weber Smokey Mountain, as you will not need it for the grilling setup. Start with the top and bottom vents fully open until you reach 300°F (149°C). Once you reach that point, you can control the temp by closing the bottom vents to bring the temperature down or opening them to bring the temperature up.

TRAEGER TIMBERLINE 1300 (PELLET GRILL)

The Traeger grill is the easiest grill with which to achieve and maintain a consistent temperature. You do not have to do anything to switch between an indirect cooking setup (smoking) or a direct cooking setup (grilling). The design of this grill is such that the insulation holds temperature well, while the precision instrumentation dials in to the exact temperature you want. As with any cooker, there are some variables to manage before you start cooking. First, it is important you check the drip tray and grease management system to ensure you have cleaned out any and all grease from your last cook. Doing this before every cook will ensure there are no flare-ups or grease spills during the cook.

Shown are three popular grills, from left to right: Big Green Egg (kamado grill), Traeger Timberline (pellet grill) and Weber Smokey Mountain (bullet grill).

Next, fill the pellet hopper with your desired wood pellets. The Traeger works as an auger, pulling the wood pellets from the hopper to the fire pot underneath the grease drip tray. The fire pot constantly burns the pellets for the duration of your cook, ensuring you get that wood-fired taste every time. Next, to get the temperature you want, simply set the temperature, hit ignite and wait for the desired temperature to be achieved. You can even set the temp from an app on your smartphone!

There are two additional considerations when cooking with a Traeger: "super smoke" setting and knowing how to get a good sear when grilling meats or vegetables.

"SUPER SMOKE"

For Traeger grills built with their smoke science technology, you can use the super smoke setting, which is a feature in their Ironwood and Timberline grill series. Super smoke uses their precision fan control to blast 100 percent hardwood smoke from the wood pellets burning inside the fire pot onto your meat in the 165 to 225°F (74 to 107°C) range. I typically start my longer cooks using this setting to maximize smoke flavor during the first 3 hours of the cook, then increase the temperature after that to make up for the added cooking time.

GETTING A SEAR

Even though you are not grilling over direct heat in a Traeger Timberline, you can still get a great sear. Once the temperature of your grill has reached 310°F (154°C) you are able to achieve the Maillard reaction. This is a chemical reaction between proteins and sugars that causes the browning you see on the surface of the meat to form, which is where so much great flavor comes from. In order to get grill marks or a full-surface sear, just get the Traeger up to 350°F (177°C). (I use this number as it is higher than 310°F [154°C] and allows for drops in temperature when opening and closing the lid.)

You can add a cast-iron pan, or a unique BBQ tool named a GrillGrate, to your Traeger's grilling surface and allow them to preheat for 30 minutes. These surfaces can get to a higher temperature, which ensures a nice, even sear. I typically grill the food for 4 minutes per side before flipping to ensure a good sear on the food. You can still get grill marks using the grilling grates that come with the Traeger Timberline, just remember to preheat the cooker to at least 350°F (177°C) before placing your food inside.

So, as you can see, cooking BBQ is much more than just wood, heat, meat and sauce. There are many factors to consider when planning your cook. But the most important fundamental to master is knowing when your BBQ is done. Let's take a look at that in the next chapter.

THE FINISH

Learn My Tips and Tricks to Serve Great BBQ Every Time

One of the things every backyard barbecuer must master is knowing when your BBQ is done. Unlike other things you have cooked, where time and temperature are the governing factors, BBQ has several other factors to consider. Simply following a recipe isn't enough to produce great BBQ. In this chapter, I will break down the seven variables you need to manage in order to know when your BBQ is ready.

The seven variables are meat selection, cooking temperature, humidity, time, internal temperature of the meat, visual cues and touch. Once mastered, you will be able to cook in any environment and to deliver great results every time. After covering each of these seven variables in depth, I will walk you through a sample recipe using a whole packer brisket, in which I put it all together for you.

MEAT/CUT	SUGGESTED TEMPERATURE	APPROXIMATE COOKING TIME
Brisket	225°F (107°C)	10–13 hours
Pork Shoulder (butt)	275°F (135°C)	8–10 hours
Ribs	250°F (121°C)	4–5 hours
Whole Chicken	225°F (107°C)	2–3 hours

VARIABLE 1. MEAT SELECTION

First, meat selection is important, since every piece of meat you will smoke will be different in size, density and quality. Considering all of those factors before your cook is the first variable to think through to help you know when your BBQ will be done.

If you are cooking beef, then grade selection is your first decision point. The higher the grade, the better the marbling, which means you will have a lot of intramuscular fat to cook with. As this fat, along with the connective tissue, breaks down during a cook, it will cool the meat from inside, creating a condition called the "stall." Basically, your meat has enough fat and collagen broken down internally to "stall" the temperature for a period of time until that cooks off and the temperature will start to rise again.

If you are cooking with a lower grade of beef such as Select or Choice you will want to consider using a lower temperature to ensure you are producing enough collagen to offset the lack of fat in the meat. In addition, using beef stock to rehydrate the brisket when wrapping can help, too.

For pork, there are many variants on the market, and it isn't graded like beef to help you figure out the quality before cooking. Look for cuts of pork that have visible fat, and for ribs look for a lot of meat on the bones. The thicker the meat for pork ribs, the better they will do during a long cook in your smoker. If the ribs are thin and less meaty, they may be dry by the time you finish cooking them. If you have inexpensive "thin" ribs, you can always cook at a lower temperature (e.g., 225°F [107°C]) and for a shorter amount of time to get better results.

Finally, picking out chicken is like pork in the sense it isn't graded like beef. However, chicken is forgiving compared to pork because most people generally do not smoke chicken for a long period of time. Keep in mind there is a big difference between organic chicken and commercially graded chicken. I find that organic chickens are substantially smaller in size and meat density than their commercially raised counterparts. This will affect the time it takes to get a chicken ready for your guests, because smaller chickens will cook much faster.

You can still get a good end result with smaller chickens by lowering the temperature and possibly the cooking time so the meat doesn't dry out. In addition, if I am cooking with a chicken like this, I will use a brine to get the final result as juicy as possible.

Bottom line: Thinking through your meat selection is an important first step when planning to have your BBQ ready at your target time.

VARIABLE 2. COOKING TEMPERATURE

As I covered in Fundamental 3: Controlling Temperature and the BBQ Zone, the temperature range for classic BBQ is between 225 and 275°F (107 and 135°C). In that range your temperature is high enough to cook the protein, but not so high that it will render the fat too quickly, resulting in dry, overcooked BBQ. Maintaining this temperature throughout the cook in combination with humidity is what enables the smoke flavor to penetrate the surface of the meat and to form that delicious bark you are looking for. Refer to Fundamental 3: Controlling Temperature and the BBQ Zone for more details on doing this effectively.

The biggest thing to keep in mind as it relates to temperature and knowing when your BBQ will be done is the effect it has on time. The higher the temperature is in the 225 to 275°F (107 to 135°C) range, the less time it will take you to get to the end result.

MEAT/CUT	END TEMPERATURE RANGE	WHERE TO MEASURE
Brisket	190–210F° (88–99°C)	Flat
Pork Shoulder (butt)	190–204°F (88–96°C)	Middle of the meat away from the bone
Ribs	190–204°F (88–96°C)	In between the bones
Whole Chicken	165–185°F (74–85°C)	In the breast/in the thigh (middle of the meat away from the bone)

VARIABLE 3. HUMIDITY

The third variable is maintaining humidity between 70 and 80 percent in your grill or smoker. As explained in Fundamental 2: Controlling Humidity, moisture is key to absorbing the gas released by the burning wood into the surface of the meat. Knowing how your smoker manages humidity and your role in that is a key factor to knowing when your BBQ will be done.

Judging when BBQ is done is comprised of tenderness, smokey flavor and a well-developed bark. Managing humidity effectively takes care of the smokey flavor and the bark. Watch how the pellicle is forming on your meat and take the steps necessary to manage that either with a spray bottle or with a mop. Your goal is to keep the surface area uniform in coloration and sticky in texture.

VARIABLE 4. TIME

When managed correctly, time will be your best friend. No matter what you are planning to cook, to get truly great BBQ, it takes time and lots of it. You need to manage your time wisely throughout the cook, paying attention to all the variables I am outlining in this chapter. Take notes every time you cook, outlining how you managed the variables and the impact it had on the final product. Time and experience will add up to you mastering the details necessary to produce the best BBQ. And the good news is, after reading this book and mastering these fundamentals, you will be well on your way to having the experience needed to be a backyard BBQ legend.

In addition, pre-planning your cook and having a game plan written down before you light your fire is important to knowing when your BBQ is done. In doing so, you are prepared to manage each aspect and are already thinking through the steps needed so when things change, you are ready and can adjust. As with the temperature variable outlined above, remember you should never cook BBQ right up to a specific time. It is safer for you to overestimate the time you need to cook the BBQ and finish early, as you can wrap the meat, place it in a cooler and rest it before your guests arrive. BBQ can rest for several hours if properly insulated and kept warm, which gives you lots of flexibility. In the table on the previous page, I give you a sense of the time it takes to smoke the most common cuts in BBQ.

Every piece of meat will cook differently and be ready at different times. So, use time as a reference point leading you to the three final variables.

VARIABLE 5. INTERNAL MEAT TEMPERATURE

The fifth variable is the internal temperature of the meat you are cooking. For instance, the USDA considers steak to be done when it measures 145°F (63°C), but a brisket will not be ready to eat at that point. To make it more interesting, there have been times when my brisket was ready at 190°F (88°C) and other times when it was ready at 204°F (96°C). So, just as we discussed with time, temperature is another data point for you to manage during the cooking process, but it isn't the only variable that lets you know when the cook is done. Outlined above is a chart with the temperature range for each of the popular BBQ cuts, so you have a reference to go by.

MEAT/CUT	TOUCH CUES
Brisket	Probe-tender in both the flat and point muscles
Ribs	The "bend" test or toothpick test
Pork Shoulder (butt)	Probe-tender in the meat
Chicken	When you probe, the juice that runs out is clear

VARIABLE 6. VISUAL CUES

As mentioned on page 25 in Fundamental 2: Controlling Humidity, watching the pellicle form is key to getting BBQ flavor. The way humidity is managed on the surface of the meat creates the environment for the gas absorption that gives BBQ its unique flavor. But that's just the start of your visual cues.

In order to know when BBQ is done, you have to form that delicious bark (a combination of a deep mahogany color and hardened texture) on the outside of the meat. A delicate dance plays out between the Maillard reaction of the meat and the caramelization of the sugars in your rub. Over time, the smoke turns the color of the bark from mahogany to a deeper color like dark chocolate. It is not uncommon for BBQ to be described as looking like a meteor. You want to see that deep color form on the surface of your pork shoulder, brisket, ribs and even chicken. Bark formation and color on your BBQ is a key variable to know when you are done.

VARIABLE 7. TOUCH

Finally, the seventh and last variable to manage is touch. This is arguably the most important factor in determining when your BBQ is ready. For brisket and pork shoulder, you want the meat to be "probe-tender." Basically, you want a meat thermometer (probe) to slide into the meat with as little resistance as possible. Think of putting a nail into a bag of gelatin.

The most common mistake when cooking BBQ is to fall into the time/temperature trap. As an example, you have been cooking a brisket for 12 hours, the temperature is reading 200°F (93°C), but when you probe the meat you are still feeling resistance, like the feeling of putting the probe in a raw piece of meat. This means the brisket is not

ready. It is ready when that probe slides in and out with no resistance. Now, the one caveat to that is that when the meat measures 210°F (99°C) and above, you are now at the point of boiling water. So, all of that rendered fat and collagen start to cook off, resulting in stringy and dry BBQ. You want to make sure you are managing that fine line and are highly tuned in to this part of the cook.

For ribs, there are several "touch" cues to let you know when they are ready, with the easiest being the bend test. Pick up the ribs with your tongs, about halfway down the rack. If the other half bends over and a crack forms in the meat, you're ready. Another method to test for doneness with ribs is the toothpick test, which works a lot like the probe-tender test for brisket and shoulder mentioned above. Put a toothpick into the rib meat between the bones—if there is little to no resistance, your ribs are ready.

In addition, the doneness of ribs means something different to many people as some like "fall-off-the-bone" ribs while others like a little "tug" to their ribs. If you serve "fall-off-the-bone" ribs to a judge in a BBQ competition, you will not get kind results.

You can reference the table above to have a guide for the most important touch cues to know when your BBQ is done.

Now that we have covered the seven variables to knowing when your BBQ is ready, let's put it all together with my brisket recipe in the next section. This recipe will walk you through smoking a whole packer brisket (the flat and the point) start to finish, highlighting the seven variables as outlined in this chapter.

PUTTING IT ALL TOGETHER

How to Smoke a Texas-Style Whole Packer Brisket

The most-asked question I get from my followers online or when I am teaching a class is how to cook a brisket. Without question, this is the number one item on every BBQ novice's wish list to master. I was there and understand how intimidating a whole packer brisket can be. It is both a large investment in time and money so just getting started is hard enough. So, I thought it appropriate to dedicate an entire chapter on smoking a whole packer brisket and to put all the fundamentals covered earlier in the book together. With that said, let's dive in by defining what a "whole packer" brisket is and how you should smoke one.

A whole packer brisket comprises two muscles that sit on top of one another separated by a layer of fat. The flat muscle (pectoralis profundus) is lean and more rectangular in shape. The point (pectoralis superficialis) is fatty and looks like a bulging mound of meat sitting on top. You can easily find brisket flats at most grocery stores, but for central Texas–style BBQ, you want a "whole packer" brisket. What makes this central Texas–style BBQ is the magic of this recipe. This brisket recipe uses a simple dry rub mix and oak wood to flavor the meat.

Note that I have given a suggested timeline that you can follow, but feel free to adapt it if you want to start the process earlier or later in the day. This timeline will allow you to have your brisket ready to serve for dinner (6:00 or 7:00 p.m.). The day starts early for a big cook like this, but trust me, after 10 to 14 hours in your smoker, this will be the best BBQ by far you have ever cooked.

TEXAS-STYLE SMOKED WHOLE PACKER BRISKET

FEEDS: 20

SUGGESTED WOOD: Oak

APPROXIMATE TOTAL COOK TIME: 10–14 hours

GRILL SETUP: Indirect

BRISKET
1 (12–15-lb [5–7-kg]) whole packer brisket

1 tbsp (15 ml) mustard

DRY RUB
¼ cup (73 g) kosher salt

¼ cup (73 g) Lawry's seasoned salt

½ cup (64 g) cracked black pepper

SPRITZ
½ cup (120 ml) water

½ cup (120 ml) apple cider vinegar

½ tsp of Worcestershire sauce

½ tsp of your favorite hot sauce

FINISH
1 cup (240 ml) beef broth

SUPPLIES NEEDED
Butcher paper

Instant-read thermometer

Spray bottle (for spritz)

3:00 A.M.: MEAT PREPARATION

Trim the fat cap of the brisket down to ¼ inch (6 mm). Trim the large chunk of hard fat that sits between the point and flat muscles on the meat side of the brisket. Trim the sides and ends to be uniform in shape.

*Trim the fat cap on the brisket to ¼"
(6 mm).*

Remove any hard fat between muscles.

*Slather all surfaces of the brisket
with yellow mustard; this will help the
spices stick better to the meat.*

*Season the brisket generously all over
with the rub.*

Coat the entire surface of the brisket with the mustard, creating a light slather to which the spices will adhere. Mix together the kosher salt, Lawry's seasoned salt and cracked pepper together in a shaker or small bowl. Now, shake the spice mix evenly across all surfaces of the brisket, or use your hand to sprinkle it evenly. (Note: You may not use all of the dry rub and can save a little to add to the brisket when wrapping.) Let the meat sit out at room temperature for at least an hour before putting it on the smoker (this allows the meat to start cooking faster at the lower temperature. If you put a large cut of meat like this in the smoker when the meat is still cold, it will add up to an hour or more to your total cook time).

4:00 A.M.: SETTING UP THE GRILL

FOR BULLET GRILLS (WEBER SMOKEY MOUNTAIN) OR KAMADO-STYLE GRILLS (BIG GREEN EGG):

Load the lump charcoal, light a small fire and preheat the cooker to 225°F (107°C). Refer to page 34 in Fundamental 3: Controlling Temperature and the BBQ Zone for more detail on setup.

★ NOTE ★

On the Big Green Egg, I like to put a small steam table pan of water on top of the grill grate to help introduce more humidity to the cook.

FOR PELLET GRILLS (TRAEGER):

Set your temperature to 225°F (107°C), and set for super smoke. Refer to page 37 in Fundamental 3: Controlling Temperature and the BBQ Zone for more detail on setup.

5:00 A.M.: PUTTING THE MEAT ON THE GRILL

Once the temperature is stable at 225°F (107°C) and you see the smoke turn from white to blueish gray, it is time to put your meat inside. Place the brisket fat side down onto the grate in the grills in which the heat source is below (i.e., bullet and kamado) or fat side up in the pellet grill. The fat cap renders slowly during the long cook and will act as a barrier between the meat and the heat source, helping to prevent the surface area from drying out.

PRO TIP

There is much debate on fat side up or down. For me, it depends on which cooker you are using. I have found when the heat source is below the meat, fat side down is the way to go, and vice versa.

5:00–8:00 A.M.: THE FIRST 3 HOURS OF SMOKING A BRISKET

For the first 3 hours of the brisket cook, leave the brisket alone. Do not open the grill for any reason! This first phase is when the pellicle is forming and the most important smoke absorption occurs. However, you do want to ensure the temperature remains consistent when using the Big Green Egg or the Weber Smokey Mountain. You can make micro adjustments up or down during this phase using the vents without interrupting the progress of the meat smoking inside. After 3 hours, that's when the fun begins.

8:00 A.M.: MANAGING THE MIDDLE OF A BRISKET COOK

As you are waiting to check in on the brisket after the 3-hour mark, now is the time to prepare a spray bottle to mist the brisket during the next part of the cook (or you could do this in a bowl and use a mop instead). Fill your spray bottle with the spritz ingredients: ½ cup (120 ml) of water, ½ cup (120 ml) of apple cider vinegar, ½ teaspoon of Worcestershire sauce and ½ teaspoon of your favorite hot sauce.

Once you have made it through the first 3 hours of the cook, it's time to check the brisket. You should have decent color forming on the outside of the meat. And you want to ensure your pellicle is not too dry or too wet. At this part of the cook, you may need to spray the outside of the brisket with the spritz liquid.

To check, open the smoker, look inside and touch the surface area of the flat part of the brisket with your fingertip. Do not move or pick up the brisket, as you do not want to interrupt the bark formation. You want the surface to be slightly sticky to the touch but not wet. If it is dry and streaky, spray the surface using the spray bottle. Remember, you do not want to overly mist the meat, as that will cause the surface area to be overly wet and will cause the bark and smoke to run off. This will help the formation of the bark more than anything else.

At this stage in the cook, most if not all of the smoke flavor has been absorbed into the meat. But the gases and oils being released from the wood smoldering inside the firebox need to adhere to the surface of the meat in order to form that dark color you want. To ensure that happens, making sure the surface area stays moist is key.

Once you've sprayed the surface of the meat (if necessary), close the cooker and let it continue smoking. You will want to check and mist the meat every 30 minutes or so until you wrap the brisket after it breaks stall (more on that later). You may not need to mist the meat each time; only do so if the surface looks and/or feels dry.

9:00–10:00 A.M.: THE STALL . . .

Brisket is a very large, dense cut of beef. Over time as it cooks slowly inside the smoker, the fat and connective tissue break down, releasing liquid in the form of rendered fat and collagen. After 4 or 5 hours of total cooking time, the internal temperature will stick at one spot, usually between 150 and 160°F (66 and 71°C). This temperature "stall" can last several hours and be frustrating.

I suggest using a digital instant-read thermometer to check the temperature of both the point and flat muscles. Make sure you are not putting the tip of the thermometer into the deckle (fat layer), as that will not give you accurate results. The best time to check the temperature is when you are looking at the brisket's bark formation every 30 minutes or so. Open your smoker, observe the bark formation, take a temperature and note the changes.

My advice to you is to wait until the brisket breaks stall (i.e., the temperature starts rising again) before wrapping. In my experience, wrapping is not designed to break the stall but rather to help tenderize the meat in the final stages of the cook. Waiting until the stall has broken helps you develop that deep, rich and dark bark you want.

Once the internal temperature starts climbing by more than a degree from the stalled temperature, and your bark is a dark mahogany color and not streaking when you mist it, it is time to take the brisket off the smoker and to wrap it.

Spritz or mop the brisket as needed throughout the cook to maintain a moist environment on the surface of the meat. This forms the pellicle, which will give you the best flavor and color.

This photo shows that the bark has formed well and is richly colored; it's ready to pull from the smoker and to wrap.

10:00–11:00 A.M.: THE WRAP (TEXAS CRUTCH)

You have a choice at this point to wrap in aluminum foil or butcher paper. To be direct, I have had success with both methods. However, I usually wrap in butcher paper now, as it gives you a slight advantage to bark formation.

Basically, paper allows the steam inside to release without getting trapped inside. This helps the bark get darker and provides the texture you want. Wrapping with foil usually speeds up the time to get the brisket probe-tender, but can negatively impact bark formation—the steam expressed from the meat has nowhere to escape and falls back as moisture on the surface, causing the bark to streak. That is why most pit masters today wrap with butcher paper.

Before you remove the brisket from the smoker, prepare two pieces of butcher paper roughly 30 inches (76 cm) long each and overlap them. (See photos on the next page.)

Carefully remove the brisket from the smoker and place it about a third of the way up the overlapping butcher paper. Spray one more time with the spritz bottle you have been using during this cook. Add a few shakes of any remaining spice mixture to the surface of the meat. Wrap up the brisket in the paper by folding the bottom of the butcher paper closest to you up and over the top of the brisket, then folding up the sides on the right and left (like you are making a burrito) and then rolling the brisket forward.

Pour 1 cup (240 ml) of beef broth in the bottom of an aluminum pan large enough to fit the brisket. Then place the wrapped brisket in the pan. Place the pan with the brisket back in the smoker and let it cook until it is done.

3:00–4:00 P.M.: HOW TO KNOW WHEN YOUR BRISKET IS DONE

From this point it is a waiting game, as the brisket will rise in temperature from 170°F (77°C) to 190 to 210°F (88 to 99°C). Here are the cues to look for and the actions to take that will help you determine when the brisket is ready to come off the cooker.

TEMPERATURE: Brisket is two muscles joined together with a thick layer of fat. One muscle is large and fatty, while the other is long, flat and lean. Both muscles will not reach the same temperatures at the same time. So, I like to take my cues from the flat, as that is the hardest part to get right. Once your flat starts measuring 190 to 210°F (88 to 99°C), you are ready to move on to the final test to know if the brisket is done.

The best way to take the temperature is to poke your probe right through the butcher paper. In fact, if putting the probe into your meat feels anything like the resistance you are feeling poking it through the paper, it is not done yet. You can alternatively pull the aluminum pan out of the cooker and crack the butcher paper, revealing the brisket for both visual and touch cues but poking through the paper works just fine. In addition, I check the temperature every 30 minutes once the internal temperature measures 190 to 210°F (88 to 99°C) to ensure I do not overcook it.

TOUCH: Now that your flat is measuring between 190 and 210°F (88 and 99°C), use the thermometer probe to check the flat and point for tenderness. You want the thermometer to go in and out of the brisket with little to no resistance. Think of it like poking a bag of mashed potatoes. That probe needs to slide in and out with ease. If you do not feel that, leave the brisket in your smoker and check every 30 minutes until that is the texture you feel when taking the temperature. Refer to Fundamental 4: The Finish (page 41) for more details on recognizing when your BBQ is done.

Once you have decided the brisket is the proper tenderness, you are done . . . but you are not ready to eat yet. Carefully remove the pan with the brisket from the smoker and get ready for it to rest.

Prepare the butcher paper wrap by placing the paper side by side and creating a folded edge.

Overlap the papers; lining up the folded edges will make for a solid seal.

Place the brisket onto the butcher paper wrap.

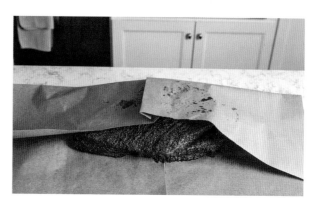

Fold the butcher paper over the brisket.

Fold the right and left ends of the butcher paper over the sides of the brisket.

Roll the brisket in the butcher paper to wrap completely and seal.

4:00–6:00 P.M.: RESTING

Now that the brisket is off the smoker, take the brisket out of the aluminum pan, pour out the beef broth and drippings from the brisket so the pan is empty and open the butcher paper wrap slightly at one of the seams, allowing heat and steam to escape. Put the semi-wrapped brisket back in the aluminum pan (to catch any drippings), and let it sit at room temperature until the internal temperature drops to 165°F (74°C) (usually 30 minutes). This stops the carryover cooking and brings the temperature of the brisket to a place that is optimal for resting.

Now, take the brisket out of the aluminum pan (tightly wrapping it in the butcher paper by closing that exposed seam) and place it on a cutting board or work surface. Wrap it in plastic wrap, then wrap that in an old towel and place it in an empty cooler for at least 2 hours and up to 4 hours. This resting is a key step to getting your brisket as juicy as possible.

6:00–7:00 P.M.: SLICING AND SERVING

Finally, when ready to serve, take the brisket out of the cooler. Remove the wrapping and place the brisket on a cutting board. Separate the point from the flat by cutting through the deckle (fatty layer between the two muscles). Now slice the flat into pencil-thin slices. The point can be cubed for burnt ends or sliced against the grain for juicy, fatty slices of brisket deliciousness.

*See a photo of the finished brisket on page 46.

PRO TIP

The reason you rest a wrapped brisket 2 to 4 hours is that the longer the brisket rests, the more the rendered fat and collagen settle and get reabsorbed into the muscle fibers as the meat cools and relaxes. This gives you all the control to serve your dinner guests the juiciest brisket ever. The sweet spot for most people is 2 hours, but you can wait an extra 2 as needed if it accommodates your serving time. You can rest it longer, but I feel the texture of the brisket suffers some when resting more than 4 hours. In addition, the reason you use a cooler is for insulation. In other words, the insulation in the cooler helps retain the temperature so the brisket does not fall below 145°F (63°C). If you have another insulated container such as a Cambro Hot Box you can use that instead of the cooler. Bottom line is, you want an insulated container to retain the heat during the rest.

BONUS TECHNIQUES

Warm Smoking, Hot Smoking and Smoke Roasting

Now that we have covered the four fundamentals of smoking as they apply to traditional BBQ, let's take a look at some other ways you can use your smoker to produce great-tasting food. In the spectrum of hot smoking foods, you have three other distinct temperature bands in which you can cook. Let's take a look at each (in the table below), then go into more detail with a few recipes putting them into practice.

WARM SMOKING

For the types of foods cooked in warm smoking, you want the temperature of your grill high enough so that you are above the food safety danger zone of 40 to 140°F (4 to 60°C), but low enough to ensure minimal evaporation of moisture or rendering of too much fat. That's the trick to warm smoking food: a balance of safety, texture and flavor.

Although you can use any type of grill for warm smoking, the Traeger Timberline grill is an ideal vehicle for this type of cooking. It is well insulated and, because it is electric, it can hold a lower temperature for a long time without issue. Although the Big Green Egg is well insulated and can also do a good job with warm smoking, you will need to focus on fire management techniques to get and hold a consistent lower temperature. The Weber Smokey Mountain can also be used, but will take lots of practice and effort because this cooker is fueled by charcoal and not insulated. More on this in the following beef jerky recipe using warm smoking.

SMOKING TYPE	TEMPERATURE RANGE	FOODS
Warm Smoking	165–180°F (74–82°C)	Jerky and bacon
Hot and Fast Smoking ("Turbo")	325–350°F (163–177°C)	Ribs, Boston butt and brisket
Smoke Roasting	350–400°F (177–204°C)	Poultry and vegetables

I love galbi, a Korean short rib dish. The marinade used to tenderize and flavor the meat is the perfect combination of sweet and savory. And because jerky is one of my favorite snacks when I need something to keep me going, I decided to use the classic galbi marinade in this beefy jerky recipe. This couldn't be any more delicious; worth every bit of the time and effort put into it!

GALBI-STYLE BEEF JERKY

FEEDS: 6–8

SUGGESTED WOOD: Oak, hickory or pecan

APPROXIMATE TOTAL COOK TIME: Up to 3 hours, plus overnight for marinating

GRILL SETUP: Indirect

½ cup (110 g) brown sugar

¼ cup (60 ml) water

2 tbsp (30 ml) mirin

½ white onion, grated

1 kiwi, grated

2 tbsp (17 g) minced garlic

1 tbsp (15 ml) sesame oil

⅛ tsp black pepper

1 (2-lb [907-g]) London broil

Mix the brown sugar, water, mirin, onion, kiwi, garlic, sesame oil and black pepper in a bowl and set aside.

Next, slice the meat as thin as possible. If you have a meat slicer, this will help tremendously. If not, you can put the London broil in the freezer for 15 minutes or so until it tightens up, then slice it with a very sharp knife as thinly as you can.

In a resealable freezer bag, combine the sliced meat and the marinade, then seal the bag, incorporating the marinade throughout the meat. Unseal just a small section, push as much air out of the bag as possible and reseal. Let the meat marinate in the refrigerator for 8 hours or overnight.

The next day, remove the meat from the marinade and discard the liquid. Pat the slices of meat dry with a paper towel and set aside.

Preheat the cooker to 170°F (77°C). If you're using a kamado or bullet grill, add two to three chunks of smoking wood to the charcoal; with a pellet grill, simply preheat the cooker, as the pellets will take care of the smokey flavor. Lay out the meat in a single layer (as neatly as possible) on the racks of your smoker. Let the beef slices cook like this for 2 to 3 hours. You can start checking the meat in your cooker after the first hour to see how it's coming along and when it is ready. The jerky is ready when it is somewhat stiff, but able to bend without breaking.

Remove the jerky when it is finished cooking and let cool in an open container for 30 minutes. Store leftovers in an airtight container in the fridge.

HOT AND FAST SMOKING

The hot and fast smoking method of BBQ has some big proponents out there, namely Myron Mixon. This style of cooking will get you BBQ in roughly half the time as traditional low and slow BBQ, but it isn't without risk. If not properly managed you will end up with overcooked, dry and charred meat. I highly recommend mastering low and slow before trying this. Once you have some solid experience with low and slow, and can actively manage the cook, you can perfect this method as well. For hot and fast BBQ you will cook in the 300 to 350°F (149 to 177°C) range.

Remember from Fundamental 3: Controlling Temperature and the BBQ Zone (page 29), how cooking low and slow allows the collagen and fat to break down evenly as the energy transfers from the outer layers of the meat to the inside? Well, cooking hot and fast will greatly impact that dynamic. How you manage this change will affect the way your BBQ turns out.

First, think about the quality and cut of meat you want to cook this way. You want larger cuts with lots of fat content throughout, which for beef means Prime rating or above.

Next, do not trim as much fat from the meat as you would normally. This will allow some additional insulation and protection from the higher heat in your cooker.

When you place the meat inside the smoker, do it with the fat side of the meat pointing toward the heat source during the cook to act as additional protection from the heat. This means the fat side is pointing down in the kamado and bullet grills and pointing up in a pellet grill.

Finally, you will need to actively monitor the moisture and to add some when and where it is needed more so than with your normal BBQ cook. For example, spritzing earlier in the cook as the surface of the meat starts to dry out, refilling the water pan as needed and adding in moisture when you wrap after breaking stall. As we covered on page 24 in Fundamental 2: Controlling Humidity, you can add moisture with a spray or mop while the meat is cooking.

The biggest advantage of hot and fast cooking as it pertains to BBQ is getting to the final product much faster than traditional low and slow methodology. I will cover the best cuts to cook using this method, point out any challenges you may face and then wrap it up with a sample recipe.

Pork shoulder (Boston butt) is the best to cook hot and fast as the meat is incredibly fatty, thus more forgiving with higher heat. What I typically see go wrong in hot and fast cooks using pork shoulder is the bark getting overcooked and charred. Moving the meat around during the cook to manage hot spots and spritzing often can help with this. In addition, you chop up all the meat in the end, so the bark isn't as important as it is for brisket or ribs.

Brisket is not as fatty as pork shoulder and, as a result, needs more attention with hot and fast cooking. The part I most often have trouble with during a hot and fast brisket cook is the flat, as that is the lean side of the whole packer brisket. Just as when you cook the pork shoulder, moving the meat around to manage hot spots and spritzing frequently can help solve this.

Pork ribs are the least forgiving and trickiest item to cook hot and fast style. Find the meatiest ribs you can (I typically use baby back ribs for hot and fast BBQ) to get the best results. As with the previous two items described, moving the ribs around during the cook to manage hot spots and spritzing often helps get you great BBQ at the end.

Now, let's walk through a brisket cook using this method.

This recipe will be a fun one when you are ready to give it a try. Remember to monitor this cook much more actively than you would a traditional low and slow brisket cook. However, once you have this mastered, you will be eating delicious brisket with friends and family in half the time it normally takes.

HOT AND FAST BRISKET

FEEDS: 20

SUGGESTED WOOD: Oak or hickory

APPROXIMATE TOTAL COOK TIME: 4–5 hours

GRILL SETUP: Indirect

BRISKET RUB

2 tbsp (36 g) kosher salt

2 tbsp (13 g) 16 mesh black pepper (this is a specific size the pepper is ground to and can be found online)

1 tbsp (7 g) onion powder

1 tbsp (8 g) garlic powder

1 tbsp (7 g) smoked paprika

2 tsp (4 g) ground cumin

BRISKET

1 (12–15-lb [5–7-kg]) whole packer brisket

1 cup (240 ml) beef broth

Combine all the rub ingredients together in a shaker or bowl.

Trim the brisket to remove extra fat and loose pieces of meat. However, because this is a hot and fast cook, leave most of the fat cap intact to help insulate the meat during the cook. Season the whole brisket with the brisket rub recipe and set aside, allowing the brisket to come to room temperature as you set up your smoker.

Preheat your cooker to 300°F (149°C). If you're using a kamado or bullet grill, add two or three chunks of smoking wood to the charcoal; with a pellet grill, simply preheat the cooker, as the pellets will take care of the smokey flavor.

Place the brisket in the smoker, fat side facing the heat source and cook until the internal temperature reaches 160 to 165°F (71 to 74°C), about 2 hours.

Remove the brisket from the smoker and wrap it. To wrap the brisket, place three or four long sheets of heavy-duty aluminum foil on a table and lay the brisket on top. I like to use foil for hot and fast cooks, as it is another layer of insulation protecting the outer layers of the brisket from overcooking in the higher-heat environment. Roll up the sides of the foil to form a pocket. Now pour the 1 cup (240 ml) of beef stock on and around the edges of the brisket. Seal the foil around the brisket, making sure you do not have leaks.

★ NOTE ★

As this is a hot and fast cook, your bark will form quickly because you are cooking at a high enough temperature to get the deep mahogany color you are looking for. In addition, you do not have to worry about breaking stall like you do with a traditional low and slow brisket because the bark should be nicely formed. The intent of wrapping the brisket at this stage is solely to speed up the cook and to make the brisket more tender.

(Continued)

HOT AND FAST BRISKET (CONTINUED)

Place the wrapped brisket back on the smoker and cook for an additional 2 to 2½ hours.

You will know when the brisket is done by checking for tenderness; refer back to Fundamental 4: The Finish (page 41) for help. Start checking for doneness 1 hour into this final stage.

To check for tenderness, carefully open the foil slightly and insert a digital thermometer probe into the brisket flat. If the probe feels like it is going in and out of the brisket flat with little resistance (like sticking that probe in an opened jar of creamy peanut butter), it is ready. If the brisket is still tough, re-seal the foil and repeat the test every 30 minutes until you reach the desired state. Your target internal temperature is between 204 and 210°F (96 and 99°C) if and when the brisket is probe-tender. If you hit the desired temperature range but the brisket is still not tender, it is better to go over the desired end temperature to achieve the tenderness you associate with brisket.

When the brisket has achieved both tenderness and temperature it is time to remove it from your cooker and slightly open the foil to vent for 5 to 10 minutes. Then wrap the brisket tightly and let it rest for at least 2 hours before slicing.

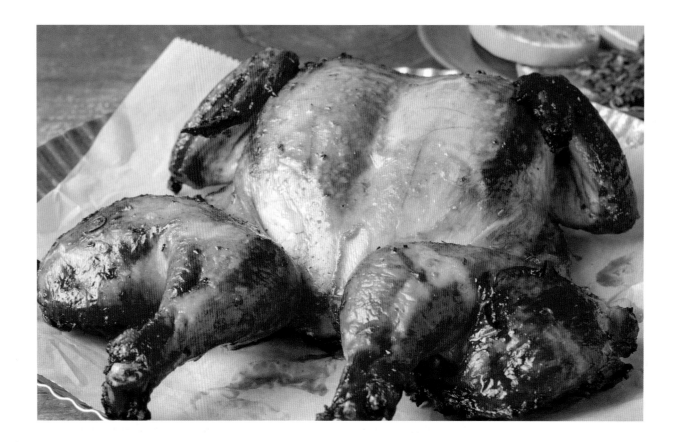

SMOKE ROASTING

Somewhere between the low BBQ Zone temperatures and the high grilling temperatures (needed for burgers and dogs) sits the "roasting zone" where temperatures are between 350 and 400°F (177 and 204°C). In this zone, you have high enough heat to get a crispy char and color on your meat, vegetables and other foods like starches, potatoes and baked goods, but low enough to cook for a length of time that allows for some smoke penetration. This is the perfect scenario to use those wood chips discussed on page 17 in Fundamental 1: Fuel, Combustion and Wood.

The key to cooking a great chicken is crispy skin! You can't achieve crispy skin when cooking low and slow, because the heat is too low for the fat to properly render from the chicken skin. Similarly, with vegetables, they're best when their skin is charred.

To get crispy chicken skin and charred vegetables, your temperature needs to be at least 350°F (177°C). Why that temperature you ask? To get that delicious color on your roasted food you need to have the Maillard reaction. This is the chemical reaction between the amino acids and the sugars in food that give browned food that amazing flavor. This reaction happens at 310°F (154°C), but (as not all temperature gauges are calibrated the same) a safe temperature to ensure the reaction happens is 350°F (177°C).

As most foods cooked using this method have a lot of moisture content (usually vegetables or chicken), you can be assured you will have enough moisture to absorb smoke flavor during the cooking process. As the food cooks, water will be evaporated, creating the humidity needed to absorb the gases released from the wood burning below. You may not be able to develop the deep color and flavor of other smoked foods in this book using this method, but you will be able to impart just enough smoke flavor to know this was cooked over an open fire.

ZESTY LEMON AND GARLIC SPATCHCOCK CHICKEN

The flavors of this chicken dish really pop. Fusing flavors from Asian cuisine with fresh lemon and thyme gives a nuanced and layered taste sensation. Serving a spatchcock chicken to your dinner guests looks great and makes for a fantastic presentation.

FEEDS: 2–4

SUGGESTED WOOD: Apple, pecan or hickory

APPROXIMATE TOTAL COOK TIME: 1½ hours, plus 8–12 hours to marinate

GRILL SETUP: Indirect

---

1 (4–5-lb [1.8–2.5-kg]) whole chicken

10 cloves garlic, minced

4 chiles, sliced thin

1 (3-inch [8-cm]) piece of ginger, grated

1 cup (240 ml) olive oil

½ cup (120 ml) soy sauce

¼ cup (60 ml) rice wine vinegar

¼ cup (50 g) sugar

3 tbsp (45 ml) fish sauce

1 tbsp (18 g) salt

6 sprigs of thyme

2 lemons, sliced into ¼-inch (6-mm) rounds

Take the chicken out of the packaging and pat it dry with paper towels. Next place the chicken on a cutting board with the legs pointing toward you, breast side down. Use kitchen shears to remove the backbone by cutting along the backbone on both sides. You can reserve the backbone for stock if you like. Flip the chicken over so the breast is facing up toward you and use your hands to press down firmly, breaking the sternum and flattening the chicken like an open book.

Mix the garlic, chiles, ginger, olive oil, soy sauce, rice wine vinegar, sugar, fish sauce and salt in a bowl. Place the chicken in a large resealable bag with the thyme and lemons. Pour in the marinade. Place the chicken in the fridge to marinate for 8 to 12 hours.

Take the chicken out of the marinade, discard the marinade and let the chicken come up to room temp while you prepare the smoker.

Preheat the cooker to 350°F (177°C). If you're using a kamado or bullet grill, add a handful of wood chips to the charcoal; with a pellet grill, simply preheat the cooker, as the pellets will take care of the smokey flavor. Cook the chicken for 1 hour, then start checking the internal temperature of the chicken to see if the internal temperature of the breast measures 165°F (74°C). If the chicken is not done yet, cook another 20 minutes, then check the temperature again.

Once the chicken has reached an internal temperature of 165°F (74°C), remove it from the smoker and let it rest for 10 minutes before carving and serving.

*See photo on page 62.

PART 2

THE RECIPES

THINGS THAT GO "MOO" (. . . AND "BAA")

Beef is an important ingredient in BBQ around the world. Many factors go in to cooking beef to produce the best possible outcome. By this point in the book, you can now draw on what you have learned and see the fundamentals at work in real time. Cooking these recipes will help you master this ingredient and truly make it sing. In addition, as I live in Kentucky, mutton is the predominant meat used here, so you get a bonus recipe showing you how I make my version of classic Kentucky BBQ (page 77).

This dish was made famous in Texas BBQ joints. Typically, it is the actual burnt ends from the point muscle of a brisket that the pit masters trimmed off after the long smoke and served as a treat to customers waiting in line to be served. Well, you can take the whole brisket point and cube it up to make this dish and get many more bites than just one or two while waiting in line. If you can find a butcher who will sell you just the brisket point, great. If not, you can separate the brisket point from the flat and reserve the flat for another cook.

BRISKET BURNT ENDS

FEEDS: 10–12 as an appetizer

SUGGESTED WOOD: Oak or hickory chunks

APPROXIMATE TOTAL COOK TIME: 12–14 hours

GRILL SETUP: Indirect

SPRITZ

½ cup (120 ml) apple cider vinegar

½ cup (120 ml) water

1 tsp Worcestershire sauce

1 tsp hot sauce

BRISKET

1 (6–8-lb [2.7–3.6-kg]) brisket point

2 tsp (6 g) kosher salt

2 tsp (4 g) coarse black pepper

2 tsp (6 g) garlic powder

1 cup (240 ml) Kansas City–style BBQ sauce

½ cup (110 g) dark brown sugar

4 tbsp (57 g) butter, divided into small pats

Preheat your cooker to 250°F (121°C). If you're using a kamado or bullet grill, add two or three chunks of smoking wood to the charcoal; with a pellet grill, simply preheat the cooker, as the pellets will take care of the smokey flavor. Combine the ingredients for the spritz in a spray bottle, or in a bowl if you plan to mop, to use during the cook. Set it aside.

If you are starting with a whole packer brisket, separate the point from the flat by running a knife through the vein of hard white fat between the two muscles. Trim up your brisket point by removing any remaining hard fat and trimming the top fat cap down to a ¼-inch (6-mm) thickness.

Combine the salt, pepper and garlic powder in a shaker or small bowl. Sprinkle the rub liberally on all sides of the brisket point.

Place the seasoned brisket point on your smoker, close the lid and cook undisturbed for 3 hours, maintaining the temperature at 250°F (121°C).

After the first 3 hours of the smoking period, check the meat every hour. Does the pellicle look and feel slightly wet and tacky? If so, you're on the right path. If not, go ahead and spritz or mop dry spots with the cider vinegar and Worcestershire mixture. Make sure you focus on the fundamentals I have taught you to know when and where to add moisture to the meat cooking. Continue smoking until the internal temperature of your meat reads 165°F (71°C), which typically takes 6 to 8 hours.

Once the bark is set and your brisket reaches 165 to 170°F (71 to 77°C), remove the brisket point to a cutting board and wrap it in butcher paper. Return the wrapped meat to the smoker. Continue smoking until the internal temperature reaches 185 to 195°F (85 to 91°C). This typically takes another 3 hours.

Remove the meat to a cutting board and unwrap it from the butcher paper, draining any liquid from the paper into an aluminum pan. Cut the brisket point into cubes, about 1½ inches (3.8 cm) thick. Place the cubes into the aluminum pan. Toss with the BBQ sauce and brown sugar, then top with the pats of butter.

Set the uncovered pan of burnt ends back on the smoker and close the lid. Continue smoking at 250°F (121°C) for 1 to 2 more hours, or until the burnt ends have absorbed the BBQ sauce and caramelized on all sides. Remove the burnt ends from the smoker and serve.

"NO WRAP" SMOKED BEEF SHORT RIBS

Beef plate ribs are taken from the "short plate" section of a cow (the sixth through tenth rib of a cow). As a result, these ribs are called "short ribs" not for their size, but rather from the location of the cow from which they are taken. This is one of my favorite cuts of beef to smoke and surely will be one of yours, too. This recipe is easy because you will not be wrapping the ribs, instead letting them cook until tender and juicy.

FEEDS: 6–8

SUGGESTED WOOD: Oak, hickory or pecan chunks

APPROXIMATE TOTAL COOK TIME: 5–6 hours

GRILL SETUP: Indirect

DRY RUB
¼ cup (73 g) Lawry's seasoned salt

1 tbsp (6 g) black pepper

2 tsp (6 g) garlic powder

1 tsp chili powder

1 tsp onion powder

SPRITZ
1 cup (240 ml) apple cider vinegar

1 cup (240 ml) water

BEEF RIBS
1 (7-lb [3-kg]) set of beef plate ribs

1 tbsp (15 ml) yellow mustard

Mix together the dry rub ingredients in a small bowl and set aside. Combine the ingredients for the spritz in a spray bottle, or in a bowl if you plan to mop. Set it aside.

Take the beef ribs out of the refrigerator an hour before you plan to smoke them. Trim as much of the fat cap from the fatty side of the ribs as you can. For these ribs, leave the membrane intact to help keep the ribs from falling apart during the long cook.

Slather the ribs all over with a thin layer of the yellow mustard. Apply the dry rub evenly to all surfaces. Set the beef ribs aside while you preheat your cooker to 250°F (121°C). If you're using a kamado or bullet grill, add two or three chunks of smoking wood to the charcoal; with a pellet grill, simply preheat the cooker, as the pellets will take care of the smokey flavor.

Place the rack of beef ribs bone side down into your smoker. Let the ribs cook undisturbed for 3 hours, maintaining the temperature at 250°F (121°C). This will allow the pellicle to form and the ribs to take on the flavor from the wood smoldering inside.

At the 3-hour mark, open the smoker and check the ribs to see how the color and pellicle are forming. Spray or mop with the spritz mixture if needed to address dry areas. Make sure you focus on the fundamentals I have taught you to know when and where to add moisture to the meat cooking. Continue cooking the ribs, checking them every 30 to 45 minutes and spraying/mopping as needed.

At the 5-hour mark, check the ribs for bark formation and tenderness with the "bend test" (refer back to page 44 in Fundamental 4: The Finish for details). Typically, the temperature will be 190 to 204°F (88 to 96°C). If the ribs are not yet probe-tender and do not pass the bend test, continue cooking and checking them every half hour. Once the probe slides in and out of the meat with little resistance and passes the bend test, your ribs are ready.

Remove the ribs to a cutting board and let them rest for 20 minutes before slicing and serving.

Picanha (also known as culotte) is a very popular cut of beef these days. It was mainly popularized by Brazilian steakhouses (*churrascarias*) and their servers walking around with this cut on a rotisserie skewer. Fortunately, you do not have to own a rotisserie to cook this. This recipe will get you the same deliciousness that you can then cut into steaks and serve with fresh chimichurri sauce.

In addition, I am introducing a new cooking technique for you in this recipe: reverse searing. Using this style of cooking, you cook the meat at a low temperature until the internal temperature is 10°F (5°C) lower than your desired serving temperature. Then you increase the temperature of your grill (or change to a direct cooking setup for charcoal grills) and finish the cook with a sear. Now you have a perfectly cooked inside, a delicious crust on the outside and your meat has already rested while increasing the temp of the cooker!

REVERSE-SEARED PICANHA
WITH ROSEMARY CHIMICHURRI

FEEDS: 8–10

SUGGESTED WOOD: Mesquite, pecan or oak chips

APPROXIMATE TOTAL COOK TIME: 45 minutes

GRILL SETUP: Indirect, then direct

ROSEMARY CHIMICHURRI
1 shallot, minced

1 tsp red pepper flakes

4 cloves garlic, minced

½ cup (120 ml) red wine vinegar

1 tsp kosher salt

½ cup (14 g) chopped rosemary

¼ cup (15 g) chopped parsley

3 tbsp (11 g) fresh oregano

½ cup (120 ml) extra-virgin olive oil

PICANHA
2 tbsp (36 g) kosher salt

2 tbsp (13 g) coarse black pepper

2 tbsp (17 g) garlic powder

1 (2½-lb [1-kg]) picanha roast

First, make the chimichurri to allow the flavors to meld while you cook the meat. Combine the shallot, red pepper flakes, garlic, vinegar and salt in a bowl and let it sit for 10 minutes. Next stir in the rosemary, parsley and oregano, then whisk in the oil to combine the ingredients. Cover and chill for 3 hours or overnight.

To make the picanha, combine the salt, black pepper and garlic powder in a small bowl to make the rub. Preheat your cooker to 250°F (121°C). If you're using a kamado or bullet grill, add a handful of wood chips to the charcoal; with a pellet grill, simply preheat the cooker, as the pellets will take care of the smokey flavor. While the cooker is coming to temperature, trim the silver skin and extra fat off the meat side of the picanha. Crosshatch-cut the fat cap side and work the rub in to the fat cap and on the meat side.

Add the roast to the cooker and cook until the internal temperature is 120°F (49°C), 30 to 40 minutes. Pull out the meat and let it rest for 10 minutes or longer while you set up the charcoal grill to a direct setup and increase the temperature of your cooker to 450°F (232°C). For charcoal grillers, do this by opening the vents to match the grilling setup of your cooker outlined on page 34 in Fundamental 3: Controlling Temperature and the BBQ Zone. For pellet grills, change the temperature and let the meat rest while it is coming up to its final temperature.

Grill the picanha roast fat side down for approximately 90 seconds, then fat side up for approximately 90 seconds. It is worth noting that at this point your meat is already cooked, and you are looking to add a deep char and crust to the outside for that extra punch of flavor.

Pull out the roast, place it on a cutting board, slice and serve with the rosemary chimichurri.

CEDAR PLANK BACON-WRAPPED MEATLOAF

This was a fun recipe to create! I took my mother's base recipe for meatloaf and mixed it up a bit. I added some new ingredients for a modern approach, wrapped it in bacon and placed it on a cedar plank for that kiss of smoke flavor. I hope your family will love this recipe as much as mine does.

FEEDS: 8–10
SUGGESTED WOOD: Cedar plank
APPROXIMATE TOTAL COOK TIME: 1–1½ hours
GRILL SETUP: Indirect

1 tbsp (15 ml) extra-virgin olive oil

1 medium onion, chopped

¼ cup (31 g) diced water chestnuts

3 cloves garlic, minced

1 tsp dried oregano

1 tsp chili powder

1 tsp cumin

1 cup (113 g) shredded sharp cheddar cheese

¼ cup (20 g) shredded Parmesan cheese

½ cup (63 g) flour

2 eggs

1 tbsp (15 ml) low-sodium soy sauce

Kosher salt

Freshly ground black pepper

2 lbs (907 g) ground beef

6–8 slices thick-cut bacon

½ cup (120 ml) your favorite BBQ sauce (or use the Cherry Coke BBQ Sauce recipe on page 90)

Heat the olive oil in a saucepan over medium heat, then sauté the onion, water chestnuts and garlic for 2 to 3 minutes until fragrant. Add the oregano, chili powder and cumin, then mix well. Take the onion mixture off the heat and set aside. Mix the remaining ingredients (except for the bacon and BBQ sauce) in a large bowl, then add in the onion mixture, mixing well.

Soak the cedar plank for 30 minutes before cooking with it. Meanwhile, preheat your cooker to 350°F (177°C). Add the cedar plank to the grill and heat one side of the plank for 10 minutes. This is the side you will place the meatloaf on.

Remove the plank from the grill and form a loaf using the ground beef mixture. Place the bacon slices over the top of the loaf, wrapping and tucking the bacon under the loaf. Next, place the loaf on top of the cedar plank. Add the cedar plank with the meatloaf to the cooker and let cook for 50 minutes. Brush the BBQ sauce on top of the bacon-wrapped meatloaf and let cook another 10 minutes until the sauce sets.

Remove the cedar plank with the meatloaf from the cooker and let it rest for 10 minutes before slicing and serving.

SMOKED LEG OF LAMB
WITH KENTUCKY BLACK BBQ SAUCE

The one BBQ item made famous in Kentucky is smoked mutton. Mutton is an older sheep, making it much less tender and a prime candidate for a low and slow BBQ cook. Even though it is a famous dish from the area I live in, it is impossible to find mutton to use. Most of it goes to Owensboro, Kentucky, and the two famous spots for this regional BBQ dish: Moonlite Bar-B-Q Inn and Old Hickory Bar-B-Q. So for this dish I used a leg of lamb and made my own version of the classic BBQ sauce paired with it.

FEEDS: 12–16
SUGGESTED WOOD: Oak, hickory or pecan chunks
APPROXIMATE TOTAL COOK TIME: 5–7 hours
GRILL SETUP: Indirect

KENTUCKY BLACK BBQ SAUCE
1 cup (240 ml) water

2 tbsp (30 ml) distilled white vinegar

¼ cup (60 ml) Worcestershire sauce

1 tbsp (14 g) light brown sugar

1 tsp lemon juice

⅛ tsp ground black pepper

¼ tsp sriracha sauce

⅛ tsp ground nutmeg

⅛ tsp onion powder

⅛ tsp garlic powder

¼ tsp kosher salt

SPRITZ
½ cup (120 ml) apple cider vinegar

½ cup (120 ml) water

1 tsp Worcestershire sauce

1 tsp hot sauce

1 cup (240 ml) beef broth

LEG OF LAMB
1 (3–4-lb [1.4–1.8-kg]) leg of lamb

¼ cup (60 ml) yellow mustard

1 tbsp (6 g) your favorite steak rub (I recommend Dizzy Pig Cow Lick seasoning)

1 cup (240 ml) beef broth

Mix all the BBQ sauce ingredients together in a saucepan and heat over medium-high heat until they come to a simmer. Mix completely, ensuring all the ingredients are combined. Take off the heat and set aside. This sauce can be made up to a week ahead of time. If making ahead, allow the sauce to cool, then pour in a container, cover and store in the fridge.

Mix together the ingredients for the spritz in a spray bottle, or in a bowl if you plan to mop. Set it aside.

Trim the leg of lamb of excess fat and any silver skin. Apply about ¼ cup (60 ml) of yellow mustard, enough to slather thinly across the surface of the lamb leg. Rub with the seasoning, covering the entire leg of lamb.

Preheat your cooker to 250°F (121°C). If you're using a kamado or bullet grill, add two or three wood chunks to the charcoal; with a pellet grill, simply preheat the cooker, as the pellets will take care of the smokey flavor.

Place the leg of lamb inside and smoke for 4 hours, maintaining the temperature at 250°F (121°C). After the first 2 hours, open the cooker and start checking the meat for pellicle formation, doing this every 45 minutes until the next step. Every time you check the meat, ask yourself: Does the pellicle look and feel slightly wet and tacky? If so, you're on the right path. If not, go ahead and spray or mop the ribs with the spritz liquid. Remember to focus on the fundamentals I have taught you to know when and where to add moisture to the meat.

At the 4-hour mark, the lamb should have an internal temperature of 140 to 150°F (60 to 66°C). If it doesn't, leave it in until it does. Once it reaches 140°F (60°C), remove the lamb from the cooker and place in an aluminum pan, adding the beef broth to the bottom. The broth should submerge a third of the lamb. Cover the pan tightly with foil and place the pan in the cooker. Cook another 1½ to 2 hours, turning the lamb once halfway through, to expose more of the surface to the braising liquid. When the internal temperature is 200°F (93°C) and the lamb is probe-tender, it is time to remove.

Pull the pan carefully from the smoker and place it on a cutting board. Crack the foil, letting the steam escape and let it rest for 30 minutes. When it's ready to serve, you have the option of shredding the meat or serving the lamb whole and carving it. Either way, pour the Kentucky Black BBQ Sauce over the meat and serve.

SMOKED CHUCK ROAST BRAISED

WITH RED WINE AND CIPOLLINI ONIONS

This recipe fuses two of my favorite things into one dish: smoked meat and comfort food. I took my go-to pot roast recipe and jazzed it up with cipollini onions, which literally translate to "little onions" in Italian. Smoking the chuck roast first adds a depth of flavor that pairs nicely with the sweet and mild flavor of the onions. Serve this with some crusty bread and a bottle of good red wine.

FEEDS: 10–12
SUGGESTED WOOD: Oak or hickory chunks
APPROXIMATE TOTAL COOK TIME: 7–8 hours
GRILL SETUP: Indirect

CHUCK ROAST

1 tsp kosher salt
1 tsp black pepper
1 tsp garlic powder
1 (3-lb [1.4-kg]) chuck roast

BRAISE

1 tbsp (15 ml) olive oil
½ yellow onion, chopped
1 carrot, diced
3 cloves garlic, chopped
2½ tbsp (20 g) all-purpose flour
2 cups (480 ml) hearty red wine
1½ cups (360 ml) beef stock or broth
1 tbsp (15 ml) tomato paste
½ tbsp (3 g) minced fresh rosemary
1 bay leaf
1 tsp kosher salt
1 lb (454 g) cipollini (or pearl) onions, peeled

Mix together the salt, pepper and garlic powder in a small bowl.

Preheat your cooker to 225°F (107°C). If you're using a kamado or bullet grill, add a handful of wood chips to the charcoal; with a pellet grill, simply preheat the cooker, as the pellets will take care of the smokey flavor. Rub the chuck roast all over with the spice mixture.

Place the roast in your cooker and smoke it until you have an internal temperature of 160°F (71°C). Typically this takes 3 to 4 hours. (For this cook you are looking to get the smoke flavor into the chuck roast prior to adding it to the braising liquid. So, bark formation isn't the important factor to monitor for this recipe, as the beef will be submerged in the liquid soon.) Take the roast out and let it rest while you make the braise.

In a Dutch oven, heat the oil over medium-high heat. Add the onion and carrot and cook, stirring occasionally, until the onion softens, about 5 minutes. Add the garlic and cook until fragrant, about 1 minute.

Mix in the flour and stir thoroughly. Whisk in the wine a little at a time, then pour in the beef stock and whisk to incorporate. Stir in the tomato paste, rosemary, bay leaf and salt. This will thicken more when the chuck roast is cooking in this mixture.

Add the chuck roast to the Dutch oven. The roast should be barely covered with liquid. Add hot water as needed. Bring the liquid to a boil, then remove the Dutch oven from the heat, cover the pot and place the Dutch oven with the roast in the cooker.

Cook for 2 hours, checking on the roast every 30 minutes and basting any exposed meat or turning slightly to ensure all sides are being braised. After 2 hours, add the cipollini onions and cook another 30 minutes or so, until the chuck roast measures an internal temperature of 205°F (96°C) and is very tender.

Remove the roast from the liquid, transfer it to a deep serving platter (don't worry if the meat falls apart) and tent it with aluminum foil to keep it warm. Let the cooking liquid stand for 5 minutes, then discard the bay leaf. Pour the braising liquid and vegetables around the roast and serve.

SOUS VIDE SMOKED BRISKET FLAT

This is a fun way to do a brisket flat, as it fuses modern cooking techniques with low and slow BBQ. The key to this recipe is to cook the brisket flat in the sous vide bath long enough to break down the collagen and fat inside, giving you the feel and texture you expect from a sliced brisket flat. Then you add smoke flavor with a shorter cook on your smoker. This is a long and involved cook, so do it when you feel like trying something different and experimenting.

FEEDS: 10–12
SUGGESTED WOOD: Oak or hickory chunks
APPROXIMATE TOTAL COOK TIME: 32 hours, plus overnight for dry brining
GRILL SETUP: Indirect

---

1 (6–8-lb [3–4-kg]) brisket flat

Kosher salt

16 mesh black pepper (this is a specific size the pepper is ground to and can be found online)

The day before you want to cook the brisket, trim the fat cap so there is a ¼-inch (6-mm) layer left and trim away the silver skin. Rub with kosher salt (about ½ teaspoon per pound [454 g]) all over. Place on a wire rack on a sheet pan and let it rest in the fridge overnight. Some folks call this "dry brining"; the process of salting large cuts of meat like this before you cook helps with denaturing and tenderizing the meat.

The next day, take the brisket flat out of the fridge and place it in a plastic bag. Next, vacuum seal the bag of brisket. (Divide into smaller sections if your sous vide cooker will not fit the whole flat.) Preheat your sous vide cooker to 155°F (68°C) and place the bag (or bags) into it, ensuring they are completely submerged. Let this cook for 30 hours. The brisket will naturally come up to 155°F (68°C) in the sous vide cooker.

After 30 hours, preheat your cooker to 250°F (121°C). If you're using a kamado or bullet grill, add two or three wood chunks to the charcoal; with a pellet grill, simply preheat the cooker, as the pellets will take care of the smokey flavor. Next, take your brisket out of the vacuum-sealed bag. Reserve the liquid. (If you want to reuse it later for a sauce, you can warm it and drizzle over the brisket when served.) Dry the brisket off with paper towels. Cover the brisket flat with 16 mesh black pepper, usually about 3 tablespoons (19 g), depending on the size of the brisket.

Place the brisket into your smoker and cook for up to 2 hours. The reason for the 2-hour time limit is that the brisket has already been fully cooked, so you are simply looking to add smoke flavor and color to the brisket flat. Exposing the cooked flat to 2 hours of smoke in your cooker is enough time to do that. After you pull the brisket flat from your cooker, slice it against the grain and serve.

REVERSE-SEARED KOREAN MARINATED TRI-TIP

When it comes to cooking beef, the flavors of Korean cuisine pair perfectly with any cut. For this recipe, I incorporated some of my favorite elements of Korean beef dishes and paired them with a tri-tip roast. Tri-tip is a cut from the bottom of the sirloin section of a cow and is a popular cut on the West Coast of America. You can find them at your local butcher or order them online from Snake River Farms. Tri-tip is ideal for reverse searing. This means we will cook the meat at a low and slow temperature until it almost reaches your preferred doneness. Then we rest the steak, bump up the temp and quickly grill it to achieve that perfect flavor-packed crust with a nice pink center.

FEEDS: 6–8

SUGGESTED WOOD: Pecan, hickory or mesquite chips

APPROXIMATE TOTAL COOK TIME: 40 minutes, plus 4 to 12 hours marinating time

GRILL SETUP: Indirect, then direct

---

2 lbs (907 g) tri-tip roast

5 tbsp (75 ml) soy sauce

3 tbsp (45 g) sugar

2 tbsp (30 ml) mirin

4 tbsp (60 ml) pineapple juice

4 cloves garlic, minced

2 tsp (4 g) fresh grated ginger

1 tbsp (5 g) gochujaru pepper (or red pepper flakes)

2 tbsp (30 ml) sesame oil

¼ tsp black pepper

3 scallions, minced, plus more for garnish

Trim off the extra fat and silver skin from the tri-tip and place it in a large resealable bag.

Blend together the soy sauce, sugar, mirin, pineapple juice, garlic, ginger, gochujaru, sesame oil and black pepper in a food processor. Pour the marinade over the tri-tip in the bag, then add the minced scallions. Let the meat marinate in the fridge for at least 4 hours and up to 12 hours.

Remove the beef from the bag and let it come up to room temperature while you set up the cooker. Preheat your cooker to 250°F (121°C). If you're using a kamado or bullet grill, add a handful of wood chips to the charcoal; with a pellet grill, simply preheat the cooker, as the pellets will take care of the smokey flavor.

Cook the tri-tip for 30 minutes or until the internal temperature measures 120°F (49°C). At this point, pull out the tri-tip roast and let it rest while you set up the charcoal grills to a direct setup and bump up the temperature of your cooker to 375°F (191°C). For charcoal grillers, do this by opening the vents to match the grilling setup of your cooker outlined on page 34 in Fundamental 3: Controlling Temperature and the BBQ Zone. For pellet grillers, change the temperature and let the meat rest while it is coming up to its final temperature.

When the grill is up to 375°F (191°C), put the roast back on and let it cook until your desired doneness is achieved (125°F [52°C] for rare, 135°F [57°C] for medium-rare, 145°F [63°C] for medium). When ready, remove the meat and allow it to rest for 10 minutes. Slice against the grain, garnish with extra minced scallions and serve.

GRILLED RED CURRY FLANK STEAK

This marinated steak recipe is a big flavor bomb. The sweet, spicy and sour flavors meld together to highlight the perfectly charred meat from your grill. For added spice you can mince a jalapeño and add that or more curry paste to the marinade. I love to slice this thin and serve it in lettuce cups over cold rice noodles.

FEEDS: 4–6

SUGGESTED WOOD: Oak, mesquite or pecan chips

APPROXIMATE TOTAL COOK TIME: 10–20 minutes, plus overnight marinating time

GRILL SETUP: Direct

1½ lbs (680 g) flank steak

2 tbsp (30 ml) soy sauce

2 tbsp (30 ml) fish sauce

3 tbsp (45 g) dark brown sugar, packed

Juice and zest of 1 lime

¾ cup (180 ml) coconut milk

3 tbsp (45 ml) Thai red curry paste

Trim the excess fat and silver skin from the flank steak, then place it in a large resealable bag. Put all the remaining ingredients in a food processor or blender, and blend until smooth. Pour the marinade into the bag with the flank steak and refrigerate for 8 hours or overnight.

Preheat your cooker to 450°F (232°C). If you're using a kamado or bullet grill, add a handful of wood chips to the charcoal; with a pellet grill, simply preheat the cooker, as the pellets will take care of the smokey flavor. Meanwhile, remove the flank steak from the marinade and let it come up to room temperature.

Cook the flank steak for 4 to 5 minutes per side, or until the meat reaches your desired doneness (125°F [52°C] for rare, 135°F [57°C] for medium-rare, 145°F [63°C] for medium).

Remove the flank steak and let it rest for 10 minutes before slicing against the grain and serving.

THINGS THAT GO "OINK"

When people think of BBQ, pork is usually at the front of their minds. Pork is typically the kind of meat people new to BBQ start mastering first. Pork shoulder is a forgiving cut with lots of fat, and pork ribs take a quarter of the time to smoke compared to larger cuts such as brisket or pork shoulder. Focusing on pork first typically lays the foundation for mastering other types of BBQ. From classic North Carolina–Style Pulled Pork (page 102) to my Smoked Spareribs with Gochujang Glaze (page 98), this chapter is packed with delicious recipes that will help you take your BBQ game to the next level.

HOW TO CLEAN AND TRIM PORK RIBS

SPARERIBS

Depending on where you get your ribs you may need to trim them before you smoke them. Some butcher shops will do this for you if you ask. Other shops may sell them already trimmed up. If you find yourself with a full rack of spareribs, here is the best way to prepare them for smoking.

REMOVE THE SKIRT: Flip the ribs so the bone side is facing up toward you. The skirt is a strip of meat that runs along the membrane line on the bone side. If you do not trim this piece, it will take longer for this end to cook, as it is twice as thick. Take a knife and run it under the skirt to remove. You can save this to make stock later if you want to. Once you have trimmed the skirt, ensure the ribs are even; if not, trim them more until they are.

REMOVE THE MEMBRANE: Keeping the bone side up toward you, find the membrane. The membrane is a white film over the bone section of the rack. This membrane is a waterproof film that will keep out flavor from the rub and smoke. Take a butter knife, lift up the membrane on the third bone in, then take a paper towel and get a good grip on the membrane. Pull straight up and away from the rack of ribs.

REMOVING THE RIB TIPS: This is an area of meat above the ribs that contains cartilage and connective tissue. To find this area, try to fold the ribs onto themselves lengthwise like closing a book. Ribs don't bend but the rib tip section does and that is the part you want to cut off. It isn't necessarily a straight line, but remember if the section bends, it's coming off. Just find that line separating the ribs from the rib tips and cut away until you have just the ribs remaining. Now you are ready to smoke the ribs.

BABY BACK RIBS

These ribs are on top of the spareribs and have thick loin meat on them. Baby backs are delicious—shorter in length but fatter with meat. There is less to do to clean and prep them, but always follow these steps before seasoning them and placing in your smoker.

CLEAN THE MEAT SIDE: Trim any excess meat that hangs off the bone side. This is like the skirt on spareribs but much smaller. The concept is the same. Next, trim away any tough silver skin on the meat side.

REMOVE THE MEMBRANE: Flip to the bone side with the bones facing toward you and find the membrane. The membrane is a white film over the bone section of the rack. Take a butter knife, lift up the membrane on the third bone in, then take a paper towel and get a good grip on the membrane. Pull straight up and away from the rack of ribs.

Place the ribs bone side up. Take a knife and run it under the skirt to remove.

Keeping the bone side up toward you, use a butter knife to lift up the membrane on the third bone. Grip the membrane with a paper towel and pull straight up and away.

Find the line separating the ribs from the rib tips and cut away the tips until you have just the ribs remaining.

Now you have properly trimmed a rack of St. Louis–style spareribs!

HICKORY-SMOKED SPARERIBS
WITH CHERRY COKE BBQ GLAZE

Smoking ribs is a satisfying experience when cooking BBQ. The time it takes to prep and cook them is far less than bigger cuts of meat, with a payoff that can equal or surpass them. This is the perfect recipe to master once you get the BBQ bug. The smokey flavor of the ribs paired with the sweet tanginess of this BBQ sauce will surely make for a great eating experience.

For this recipe, I will walk you through my process of smoking spareribs, then serving them "wet" style, which means sauced at the end. I like to cut my spareribs St. Louis style, which is a way to trim a rack of spareribs so they are rectangular in shape. This uniform shape and size makes for an even surface to smoke, helping to form that pellicle and to take on the smoke flavor you are after.

FEEDS: 2–4
SUGGESTED WOOD: Hickory, cherry or apple chunks
APPROXIMATE TOTAL COOK TIME: 4–5 hours
GRILL SETUP: Indirect

DRY RUB
2 tbsp (36 g) kosher salt
2 tbsp (13 g) black pepper
2 tbsp (14 g) paprika

SPRITZ
½ cup (120 ml) apple juice
½ cup (120 ml) apple cider vinegar

CHERRY COKE BBQ SAUCE
1 (12–fl oz [354-ml]) can Cherry Coke
2 tbsp (30 ml) olive oil
¼ cup (40 g) minced onion
2 cups (480 ml) ketchup
¼ cup (55 g) brown sugar
3 cloves garlic, crushed
1 tbsp (15 ml) apple cider vinegar
1 tbsp (15 ml) tomato paste
1 tbsp (15 ml) Worcestershire sauce
1 tsp dry mustard
Freshly ground pepper, to taste

SMOKED SPARERIBS
1 rack (3–4 lbs [1.4–1.8 kg]) of St. Louis–cut spareribs
1 tbsp (15 ml) yellow mustard
2 tbsp (28 g) butter, cut into equal-sized pieces
2 tbsp (30 ml) honey
¼ cup (60 ml) apple juice

Mix the salt, pepper and paprika in a small bowl to form the rub and set aside. Mix the ingredients for the spritz in a spray bottle, or in a bowl if you plan to mop. Set it aside.

Into a small saucepan, pour the can of Cherry Coke. Bring to a boil and reduce the heat to a simmer. Reduce for approximately 10 minutes, stirring occasionally. Remove from the heat and set aside.

In a medium saucepan, heat the olive oil over medium heat, add the onion and sauté until slightly browned. Add the remaining BBQ sauce ingredients, along with the Cherry Coke reduction. Mix thoroughly and simmer for 20 minutes. You can add in some reserved drippings from the smoked spareribs (on the following page) to add some fatty, rich flavor to this BBQ sauce if desired.

Take the spareribs out of the refrigerator an hour before you plan to smoke them. Remove the membrane from the bone side of the spareribs and trim excess fat from the meat side (see page 88 for details).

Slather the ribs with the yellow mustard and sprinkle the rub on both sides of the ribs. Set them aside and preheat your cooker to 250°F (121°C). If you're using a kamado or bullet grill, add two or three wood chunks to the charcoal; with a pellet grill, simply preheat the cooker, as the pellets will take care of the smokey flavor.

Place the rack of spareribs bone side down in your smoker. Let the ribs cook undisturbed for the first hour, maintaining the temperature at 250°F (121°C). This will allow the pellicle to form and for the ribs to take on the flavor from the wood smoldering inside. After the first hour, open the cooker and take a look at your ribs. Do you see the color forming? Does the pellicle look and feel slightly wet and tacky? If so, you're on the right path. Spritz or mop any dry areas on the ribs if needed. Focus on the fundamentals I have taught you to know when and where to add moisture to the meat cooking.

At the 3-hour mark, pull out the ribs and place them meat side down on a sheet of aluminum foil. Place the pieces of butter and honey on the meat side of the ribs, then add the apple juice to the foil packet you are creating. Now wrap the ribs up and then wrap again in more foil to ensure they are sealed. Place them back into the smoker and let the ribs cook this way for 1 more hour.

After the hour, carefully remove the ribs from the foil and glaze them with some of the Cherry Coke BBQ Sauce, reserving what's left over. Put them back into the smoker and let them cook for another 30 minutes to set the glaze.

Pull out the ribs and let them rest for 10 minutes before slicing and serving. Serve with the reserved Cherry Coke BBQ Sauce and lots of napkins.

*See photo on page 86.

BOURBON-GLAZED SMOKED BABY BACK RIBS

Living in Kentucky, you develop a taste for bourbon. This recipe combines my love for bourbon with my passion for BBQ. The smokiness of the ribs pairs nicely with the vanilla and spice flavors from the bourbon. This glaze is so good you may want to make extra for a dipping sauce with the finished ribs.

FEEDS: 4–6
SUGGESTED WOOD: Hickory, apple or cherry chunks
APPROXIMATE TOTAL COOK TIME: 4½–5 hours
GRILL SETUP: Indirect

DRY RUB
2 tbsp (36 g) kosher salt
2 tbsp (13 g) black pepper
1 tbsp (7 g) paprika

SPRITZ
½ cup (120 ml) apple juice
½ cup (120 ml) apple cider vinegar

RIBS
2 racks of baby back ribs (about 1½–2 lbs [680–907 g] per rack)
1 tbsp (15 ml) yellow mustard

GLAZE
1 cup (220 g) brown sugar
½ cup (120 ml) pineapple juice
½ cup (120 ml) maple syrup
1 cup (240 ml) bourbon
¼ cup (60 ml) Dijon mustard

Combine the salt, black pepper and paprika in a small bowl for the rub and set aside. Mix the ingredients for the spritz in a spray bottle, or in a bowl if you plan to mop. Set it aside.

Preheat your cooker to 250°F (121°C). If you're using a kamado or bullet grill, add two or three wood chunks to the charcoal; with a pellet grill, simply preheat the cooker, as the pellets will take care of the smokey flavor. Trim the ribs (refer to page 88 for cleaning and prep directions for ribs). Next, slather the ribs with the yellow mustard and season with the rub. Place the ribs inside the smoker, bone side down.

Let the ribs smoke undisturbed for the first hour, maintaining the cooker's temperature at 250°F (121°C). At the 1-hour mark, open your cooker and check on the ribs. Does the pellicle look and feel slightly wet and tacky? If so, you're on the right path. If not, go ahead and spritz or mop where you see dry spots. Do this every 45 minutes until you apply the glaze. Make sure you focus on the fundamentals I have taught you to know when and where to add moisture to the meat cooking.

Combine the glaze ingredients in a saucepan, mix well and bring to a low boil. Once it starts to boil, lower the heat to medium and reduce the glaze until it is thick and easily coats the back of a spoon, about 30 minutes. Set the glaze aside and wait until the ribs are close to being done.

At the 4-hour mark, check the ribs for doneness by using the bend test (see page 44 in Fundamental 4: The Finish). Continue cooking if needed, until the ribs pass the bend test. When the ribs are ready, evenly spread the glaze on the racks of ribs and let cook for the final 30 minutes to set the glaze. Pull off the grill, let rest for 10 minutes, slice, serve and enjoy!

HOT AND FAST BABY BACK RIBS

As discussed in the Bonus Techniques section (page 58), you can cook some BBQ at a higher temperature, yielding quicker results. This recipe produces great-tasting ribs in half the time it normally takes. However, this cook is more interactive, because you will need to keep an eye on the meat to ensure it isn't drying out or overcooking.

FEEDS: 6–8

SUGGESTED WOOD: Oak, hickory or cherry chunks

APPROXIMATE TOTAL COOK TIME: 2½–3 hours

GRILL SETUP: Indirect

DRY RUB
1 tbsp (18 g) kosher salt

1 tbsp (6 g) black pepper

1 tsp paprika

1 tsp onion powder

1 tsp garlic powder

1 tsp cayenne pepper

SPRITZ
½ cup (120 ml) apple juice

½ cup (120 ml) apple cider vinegar

RIBS
2 racks of baby back ribs (about 1½–2 lbs [680–907 g] per rack)

1 tbsp (15 ml) yellow mustard

In a small bowl, combine the ingredients for the dry rub and set aside. Combine the ingredients for the spritz in a spray bottle, or in a bowl if you plan to mop. Set it aside.

Preheat your cooker to 300°F (149°C). If you're using a kamado or bullet grill, add two or three wood chunks to the charcoal; with a pellet grill, simply preheat the cooker, as the pellets will take care of the smokey flavor. Remove excess fat and pull the bone side membrane off from the ribs (see page 88 for details on cleaning and prepping ribs). Slather with the yellow mustard and season all over with the rub mix.

Place the ribs bone side down inside your smoker. Let the ribs cook for 1 hour undisturbed, maintaining the temperature at 300°F (149°C). At the 1-hour mark, open your cooker and check on the ribs. Remember, you are looking for the pellicle to look and feel slightly wet and tacky. If it doesn't, go ahead and spritz or mop dry spots with the spritz mixture. Do this every 20 minutes, mopping or spritzing as needed and keeping a close eye on bark formation. Make sure you focus on the fundamentals I have taught you to know when and where to add moisture to the meat cooking.

After 2½ to 3 hours, check the ribs to see if they are ready by using the bend test (see page 44 in Fundamental 4: The Finish). Continue cooking if necessary, checking every 15 minutes, until they pass. When they pass, pull the ribs from the smoker, let them rest for 10 minutes, slice and serve!

CHAR SIU GLAZED SMOKED SPARERIBS

Char siu translates from Chinese as "fork-roasted" after the traditional cooking method for this type of dish in Cantonese cuisine. The sauce and its distinctive red color feature Chinese five-spice powder and hoisin sauce. This glaze makes the perfect complement for smoked ribs.

FEEDS: 4–6
SUGGESTED WOOD: Apple, cherry or hickory chunks
APPROXIMATE TOTAL COOK TIME: 5–6 hours
GRILL SETUP: Indirect

DRY RUB
1 tbsp (18 g) salt

1 tbsp (6 g) black pepper

1½ tsp (4 g) garlic powder

SPRITZ
½ cup (120 ml) apple juice

½ cup (120 ml) apple cider vinegar

1 dash hot sauce

1 dash Worcestershire sauce

PORK SPARERIBS
2 racks of spareribs (about 3–4 lbs [1.4–1.8 kg] per rack)

1 tbsp (15 ml) yellow mustard

CHAR SIU GLAZE
4 tbsp (60 ml) soy sauce

½ cup (120 ml) honey

½ cup (120 ml) hoisin sauce

2 tbsp (30 ml) mirin

1 tsp salt

1 tsp white pepper

2 cloves garlic, minced

1 tsp five-spice powder

2 drops red food coloring

TO SERVE
Scallions, sliced on the bias, and sesame seeds, for garnish

Combine the dry rub ingredients in a small bowl and set aside. Combine the ingredients for the spritz in a spray bottle, or in a bowl if you plan to mop. Set it aside.

Preheat your cooker to 250°F (121°C). If you're using a kamado or bullet grill, add two or three wood chunks to the charcoal; with a pellet grill, simply preheat the cooker, as the pellets will take care of the smokey flavor. Clean the spareribs (see page 88 for cleaning and prep directions for ribs). Slather the ribs with the yellow mustard front and back, then season with the dry rub mix.

Place the ribs in the cooker bone side down and smoke undisturbed for the first 2 hours. After the first 2 hours, spritz or mop the ribs every 45 minutes until they are done, 5 to 6 hours. During this time, monitor the pellicle formation to ensure it is tacky and slightly wet. Remember this is where the magic happens, as the gases giving the ribs color and smoke flavor are absorbed through a slightly wet surface. If you see dry spots forming during this window of time, spritz or mop as needed.

While the ribs are cooking, make the glaze. Mix the soy sauce, honey, hoisin, mirin, salt, white pepper, garlic, five-spice powder and food coloring in a saucepan. Heat until it lightly boils, then reduce the heat to maintain a simmer. Let the sauce reduce for 30 minutes or so, until it thickens and coats the back of a spoon.

When the ribs pass the bend test (see page 44 in Fundamental 4: The Finish for details), remove them to a cutting board and spread the glaze evenly on the two racks, reserving some for dipping. Place the glazed ribs back on the smoker for 30 minutes to set the glaze. After 30 minutes, pull out the ribs and let them rest for 10 minutes. Garnish with sliced scallions and sesame seeds, then slice and serve.

SMOKED SPARERIBS
WITH GOCHUJANG GLAZE

Gochujang is one of my favorite flavor profiles to work with. The mixture of sweet, spicy and fermented flavors marries to form a great flavor profile for smoked spareribs. When the ribs are glazed, you can garnish with toasted sesame seeds, scallions and cilantro. These ribs are as beautiful as they are delicious. This glaze works well on chicken wings, too!

FEEDS: 2–4

SUGGESTED WOOD: Hickory, cherry or pecan chunks

APPROXIMATE TOTAL COOK TIME: 4½–5 hours

GRILL SETUP: Indirect

GOCHUJANG GLAZE

¼ cup (60 ml) gochujang hot pepper paste

2 tbsp (30 ml) soy sauce

2 tbsp plus 2 tsp (40 ml) honey

1 tbsp (15 ml) rice wine vinegar

1 tbsp (15 ml) freshly squeezed lime juice

1 tbsp (15 ml) toasted sesame oil

2 cloves garlic, minced

½ tbsp (3 g) fresh grated ginger

DRY RUB

1 tbsp (18 g) salt

1 tbsp (6 g) pepper

1½ tsp (12 g) garlic powder

SPRITZ

½ cup (120 ml) apple cider vinegar

½ cup (120 ml) beer

SPARERIBS

1 rack of spareribs, trimmed St. Louis style (about 3–4 lbs [1.4–1.8 kg])

1 tbsp (15 ml) yellow mustard

¼ cup (½ stick, 56 g) butter, divided into small pats

¼ cup (60 ml) liquid (your choice of beer, apple juice or water)

Sesame seeds and lime wedges, for garnish

Mix all the glaze ingredients together in a saucepan over medium heat. Do not bring the mixture to a boil, just warm and combine the flavors for 10 minutes. Take the sauce off the heat and pour into a container, reserving ¼ cup (60 ml) of the glaze for serving. Cover and place in the fridge until needed. This can be done several days in advance.

Combine the dry rub ingredients in a small bowl and set aside. Combine the ingredients for the spritz in a spray bottle, or in a bowl if you plan to mop. Set it aside.

Trim the ribs of extra fat, the flap and membrane (see page 88 for cleaning and prepping directions for ribs). Rub the ribs with the yellow mustard and cover with the dry rub. Let sit at room temperature while the cooker is preheating.

Set up your cooker to 250°F (121°C). If you're using a charcoal grill, add two or three wood chunks to the charcoal; with a pellet grill, simply preheat the cooker, as the pellets will take care of the smokey flavor. When ready, place the ribs bone side down into the cooker. Cook the ribs undisturbed at 250°F (121°C) for 1 hour. After the first hour, open the cooker and check your ribs. Does the pellicle look and feel slightly wet and tacky? If so, you're on the right path. If not, go ahead and spritz or mop where you see dry spots. Do this check every 45 minutes for the first 3 hours.

After 3 hours, pull out the ribs and place them meat side down on a sheet of aluminum foil with pats of butter. Next add the liquid (beer, apple juice or water) to the foil. Wrap the ribs tightly in the foil, then wrap it with another sheet of foil to secure the contents inside. Place back in the cooker for 1 more hour.

After the hour is up, remove the ribs from the foil and raise the temperature of the cooker to 275°F (135°C). For charcoal grillers, see page 34 for tips on adjusting the temperature. For pellet grillers, simply change the temp. While the cooker is heating, slather the ribs with the glaze, reserving some for dipping later. Place the ribs back in the cooker for 30 minutes to 1 hour.

When you see the meat pull from the bone and they pass the bend test (see page 44 in Fundamental 4: The Finish), it is time to remove them. Allow the ribs to rest for 10 minutes, then garnish with sesame seeds, slice and serve with lime wedges on the side.

CAJUN-STYLE SPARERIBS

WITH FRESH MANGO SALSA

Blackened ribs are good enough as-is but serve them with this sweet mango salsa and you have a perfect pairing. I went easy on the spice in this homemade Cajun blackening dry rub mix, so add more cayenne if you want to kick it up a notch.

FEEDS: 2–3

SUGGESTED WOOD: Hickory or oak chunks

APPROXIMATE TOTAL COOK TIME: 5–6 hours

GRILL SETUP: Indirect

FRESH MANGO SALSA
3 ripe mangos, diced

1 medium red bell pepper, chopped

½ cup (80 g) chopped red onion

¼ cup (4 g) fresh cilantro leaves, chopped

1 jalapeño, seeded and diced

1 large lime, juiced

⅛ to ¼ tsp salt, to taste

CAJUN DRY RUB
2 tbsp (14 g) smoked paprika

1 tbsp (5 g) cayenne powder

1 tbsp (7 g) onion powder

1 tsp garlic powder

1 tsp ground black pepper

1 tsp sea salt

½ tsp dried basil

½ tsp dried oregano

½ tsp dried thyme

SPRITZ
½ cup (120 ml) apple juice

½ cup (120 ml) apple cider vinegar

SPARERIBS
1 rack of spareribs, trimmed St. Louis style (about 3–4 lbs [1.4–1.8 kg])

1 tbsp (15 ml) yellow mustard

To make the mango salsa, mix all the salsa ingredients together in a bowl, cover and place in the refrigerator while you cook the ribs to allow the flavors to meld together.

Mix all the Cajun dry rub ingredients together in a small bowl and set aside. Combine the ingredients for the spritz in a spray bottle, or in a bowl if you plan to mop. Set it aside.

Preheat your cooker to 250°F (121°C). If you're using a kamado or bullet grill, add two or three wood chunks to the charcoal; with a pellet grill, simply preheat the cooker, as the pellets will take care of the smokey flavor. While your cooker is coming up to temperature, prep the spareribs. Remove the excess fat, the flap and membrane (see page 88 for cleaning and prep directions for ribs). Slather with the yellow mustard and apply the Cajun dry rub mix evenly to all sides of the ribs. Any extra dry rub can be stored in an airtight container and used for future cooks.

Place the ribs in the cooker and cook the ribs undisturbed at 250°F (121°C) for 1 hour. After the first hour, open the cooker and check your ribs. Look to see if the pellicle looks and feels slightly wet and tacky. If it doesn't, you can go ahead and spritz or mop where you see dry spots. Focus on the fundamentals I have taught you to know when and where to add moisture to the meat cooking. Do this check every 45 minutes for the first 4 hours.

At the 4-hour mark, start looking for doneness in the ribs by performing the bend test (see page 44 in Fundamental 4: The Finish). When they are done, pull the ribs from the cooker, slice and garnish with the fresh mango salsa.

NORTH CAROLINA-STYLE PULLED PORK

This recipe is my version of the BBQ made famous in North Carolina. This part of the United States is best known for whole hog and pork shoulder BBQ smoked over hickory wood. Pulled pork is the first thing everyone should master when they are learning the art of BBQ. This cut of meat is very forgiving, allowing you to learn without managing too many variables. There is so much intramuscular fat that this cut holds up well for a long cook. When done right, this is a delicious BBQ dish to serve and feed a lot of people.

FEEDS: 12–18
SUGGESTED WOOD: Hickory chunks
APPROXIMATE TOTAL COOK TIME: 9–10 hours
GRILL SETUP: Indirect

DRY RUB
2 tbsp (36 g) kosher salt
2 tbsp (13 g) coarse ground black pepper
1 tbsp (7 g) paprika

SPRITZ
¼ cup (60 ml) apple cider vinegar
¼ cup (60 ml) apple juice
2 dashes Worcestershire sauce
2 dashes your favorite hot sauce

BOSTON BUTT
1 (8–10-lb [4–5-kg]) bone-in Boston butt
2 tbsp (30 ml) yellow mustard

Mix together the dry rub ingredients in a small bowl and set aside. Mix the apple cider vinegar, apple juice, Worcestershire and hot sauce in a spray bottle, or in a bowl if you plan to mop. Set it aside.

Take your Boston butt out an hour before cooking it. Preheat your cooker to 250°F (121°C). If you're using a kamado or bullet grill, add two or three wood chunks to the charcoal; with a pellet grill, simply preheat the cooker, as the pellets will take care of the smokey flavor.

You'll want to crosshatch-cut the fat cap on the Boston butt with cuts about 1 inch (2.5 cm) apart, which helps the fat render and the seasoning to work its way down to the meat. If you want less fat in the final product, trim off the fat cap. Apply a thin layer of yellow mustard to all sides of the pork. Cover the entire pork shoulder evenly in the rub. Let sit at room temperature until the cooker comes up to temperature. (Note: You can do this the night before.)

Place your pork in the smoker and leave untouched for the first 3 hours, maintaining the temperature at 250°F (121°C).

After 3 hours, spray or mop the Boston butt every hour for the next 5 hours. Watch the formation of the bark and make sure when applying the mop liquid not to disrupt the bark. Apply evenly and smoothly during the cook.

At the 5-hour mark or when your pork stalls at 160°F (71°C), take your Boston Butt off the cooker. Apply a little spritz liquid to the outside of the butt and double wrap it tightly in aluminum foil to seal. Put the pork back on the cooker and bump up the temperature to 275°F (135°C). You can place the wrapped shoulder back in your cooker while temperature rises to 275°F (135°C). I like to bump up the temperature a little after the wrap to speed up the cook and to help deliver super-moist pulled pork. Let it cook another 2 hours, checking the meat every 45 minutes to see if it is probe-tender. When the thermometer probe goes in and out of the meat easily, you are ready. The internal temperature will be between 195 and 204°F (91 and 96°C).

Take the Boston butt off the cooker, make a crack in the foil to let steam escape and let the butt stop its carryover cooking, 20 to 30 minutes. Reseal the foil tightly, wrap the Boston butt in a towel, put it in a cooler and let it rest for 1 to 2 hours before pulling the meat and serving.

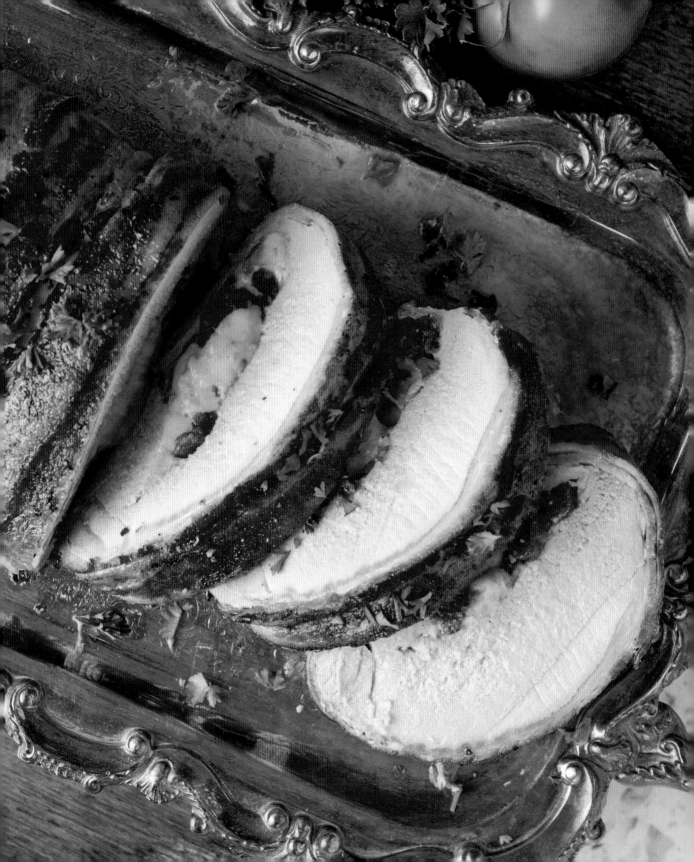

KENTUCKY HOT BROWN STUFFED PORK LOIN

As some of you know by now, I live in Louisville, Kentucky, which is the home of the famous Hot Brown sandwich. This is a must-try when visiting Louisville and is one of the best sandwiches you will ever try. Featuring tomatoes, bacon and a cheese sauce, this sandwich is hard to beat. Taking those elements and placing them in a pork loin was the inspiration here and is one of my favorite things to serve when guests are visiting us from out of town.

FEEDS: 10–12
SUGGESTED WOOD: Apple, pecan or hickory chips
APPROXIMATE TOTAL COOK TIME: 1½ hours
GRILL SETUP: Indirect

DRY RUB
2½ tsp (18 g) Lawry's seasoned salt
¾ tsp black pepper
½ tsp garlic powder
¼ tsp chili powder
¼ tsp onion powder or cumin

PORK LOIN
1 (4-lb [1.8-kg]) pork loin
Kosher salt
8 slices of Swiss cheese, cut in half
1 vine-ripened tomato, diced
10 slices of bacon
Minced parsley, for garnish

Mix together the dry rub ingredients and set aside.

First, remove the fat cap from the pork loin. Butterfly the pork loin by pressing onto the meat with one of your hands and making an even cut straight down the middle of the loin, starting at the top and ending at the bottom. Do not cut all the way through; use a light touch with your knife to slice about 2 inches (5 cm) into the meat. Open the pork loin like a book and continue making gentle cuts along the length until you are close to the opposite end of the pork loin. When you are an inch (2.5 cm) away from the other side, stop making cuts. Follow the same procedure on the other side (even if it is noticeably thicker), making gentle cuts until you are an inch (2.5 cm) away from the other side. At this point your pork loin should have the same thickness.

Now, spread out the pork loin and cover it with plastic wrap. Using a meat tenderizer, pound the meat with enough force to thin it out, but not hard enough to break the plastic. You want it to be 1 inch (2.5 cm) thick. Remove the plastic wrap and season the inside of the pork with kosher salt.

Now place slices of cheese down the middle, about one-third of the way in from the long side of the pork loin. Layer the tomatoes on top of the cheese. Grab the long end of the pork loin with the stuffing closest to it and roll up everything, tucking the ingredients inside. Wrap the outside of the pork loin with bacon by taking strips of bacon one at a time and wrapping around the circumference. Do this with all the bacon until the stuffed pork loin is fully wrapped in bacon. Cover the bacon with the dry rub. Using butcher's twine, secure the stuffed pork loin in four or five spots to ensure it stays sealed during the cook.

Preheat your cooker to 250°F (121°C). If you're using a kamado or bullet grill, add a handful of wood chips to the charcoal; with a pellet grill, simply preheat the cooker, as the pellets will take care of the smokey flavor. When ready, gently place the pork loin inside. Let it smoke undisturbed for 1 hour.

After 1 hour, bump up the temperature to 350°F (177°C). For charcoal grillers, see page 34 for tips on adjusting the temperature. For pellet grillers, simply set the new temperature. Cook the pork loin for another 30 minutes, until it measures 145°F (63°C) internally and the bacon is nice and brown.

Carefully remove the pork loin from the cooker, let it rest for 10 minutes before removing the twine, then garnish with the parsley, slice and serve.

BOURBON AND MAPLE BRINED SMOKED PORK LOIN

Pork loin is a very lean cut of pork, so to help keep it moist and flavorful for a long smoke, brining is key. This brine features two of my favorite flavors in one: maple syrup and bourbon. This is an easy and delicious meal that feeds a large crowd.

FEEDS: 10–12

SUGGESTED WOOD: Apple, pecan or hickory chips

APPROXIMATE TOTAL COOK TIME: 1–1½ hours, plus 8 hours for the brining

GRILL SETUP: Indirect

BRINE

2 cups (480 ml) water

½ cup (120 ml) pure maple syrup

½ cup (120 ml) bourbon

¼ cup (73 g) kosher salt

1 tbsp (15 ml) vanilla extract

1 tsp onion powder

1 tsp garlic powder

1 tsp black pepper

¼ tsp cinnamon

2 cups (435 g) ice

PORK LOIN

1 (4-lb [1.8-kg]) pork loin

Mix the water, syrup, bourbon, salt, vanilla, onion powder, garlic powder, black pepper and cinnamon in a saucepan over medium-high heat. Heat the brine until it simmers, letting it simmer for 1 to 2 minutes, stirring frequently, until the salt is fully dissolved. Remove the brine from the heat and add the ice to cool it down.

Prepare the pork loin. You will notice one side of the loin will have a thick layer of fat and some silver skin. Trim that off so all sides get flavor from the brine. Once trimmed, place the pork loin in a large resealable bag. When the brine is cool to the touch, pour the brine into the bag over the pork loin and place in the fridge for 8 hours or overnight.

Remove the brined pork loin and let it come to room temperature while you set up your cooker. Preheat your cooker to 250°F (121°C). If you're using a kamado or bullet grill, add a handful of wood chips to the charcoal; with a pellet grill, simply preheat the cooker, as the pellets will take care of the smokey flavor. Place the pork loin inside and cook undisturbed for 45 minutes before checking.

At the 45-minute mark, flip over the pork loin so all sides are getting even color. From this point on, keep cooking until the internal temperature is 145°F (62°C). This should take a total of 1½ hours from start to finish, but check the internal temperature at the 1-hour mark to make sure you are not overcooking.

When it's done, pull out the pork loin and let it rest for 10 minutes before slicing and serving.

BUFFALO-STYLE PORK TENDERLOIN

One of my favorite chicken wing varieties is classic Buffalo style. Spicy and tangy, they are the perfect game-day dish. This recipe fuses grilled pork tenderloin with a slightly sweeter version of Buffalo sauce. This dish makes for a beautiful presentation when serving to family or guests.

FEEDS: 2–3

SUGGESTED WOOD: Apple, pecan or cherry chips

APPROXIMATE TOTAL COOK TIME: 30–40 minutes

GRILL SETUP: Direct

PORK TENDERLOIN

1 (1½-lb [680-g]) pork tenderloin

Salt and pepper, to taste

BUFFALO SAUCE

⅔ cup (160 ml) hot sauce

½ cup (114 g) cold unsalted butter

1½ tbsp (22 ml) cider vinegar

¼ cup (60 ml) honey

¼ tsp Worcestershire sauce

¼ tsp cayenne pepper

⅛ tsp garlic powder

Kosher salt, to taste

TO SERVE

3 tbsp (24 g) crumbled blue cheese

2 tbsp (12 g) sliced celery

Preheat the cooker to 350°F (177°C). If you're using a kamado or bullet grill, add a handful of wood chips to the charcoal; with a pellet grill, simply preheat the cooker, as the pellets will take care of the smokey flavor. Trim the silver skin and extra fat from the tenderloin. Season it all over with salt and pepper.

Grill for 15 minutes, then flip and grill for another 15 minutes, or until the internal temperature measures 145°F (63°C). Remove the tenderloin and let it rest for 10 minutes.

Meanwhile, mix all the sauce ingredients in a small saucepan over medium heat until the butter has melted, the salt has dissolved and the sauce is smooth, about 10 minutes.

Slice the tenderloin and ladle the sauce all over it. Garnish with crumbled blue cheese and sliced celery.

PORK BELLY BURNT ENDS, SICHUAN STYLE

This dish has all the richness of pork belly with the comfort of your favorite Chinese takeout. You may need to visit an Asian market or to look on Amazon for some ingredients, but this dish is well worth the effort. It's a great meal to serve guests looking for something different at your next BBQ.

FEEDS: 6–8

SUGGESTED WOOD: Apple, pecan or hickory chunks

APPROXIMATE TOTAL COOK TIME: 2–3 hours

GRILL SETUP: Indirect

DRY RUB

2 tbsp (36 g) kosher salt

2 tbsp (13 g) black pepper

1 tbsp (8 g) garlic powder

SPRITZ

½ cup (120 ml) apple juice

½ cup (120 ml) apple cider vinegar

PORK BELLY

1 (1½-lb [680-g]) pork belly

1 tbsp (15 ml) yellow mustard

SICHUAN SAUCE

¼ cup (60 ml) soy sauce

1 tbsp (15 ml) distilled white vinegar

1 tbsp (8 g) cornstarch

1 tbsp (15 ml) sambal oelek

¼ cup (60 ml) Shaoxing wine (or dry sherry, if unavailable)

2 tbsp (30 g) sugar

⅓ cup (80 ml) peanut oil

2 small leeks, white and light green parts only, cut into ¼-inch (6-mm) slices (about ½ cup [45 g] total)

3 scallions, whites finely minced, greens thinly sliced on a bias and reserved for garnish

2 cloves garlic, minced

1 tbsp (6 g) minced fresh ginger

12 hot Chinese dry chile peppers, seeded

GARNISH

1 tbsp (6 g) Sichuan peppercorns, toasted in a hot skillet for 30 seconds until fragrant, then ground using a mortar and pestle

½ cup (73 g) roasted unsalted peanuts

Mix together the dry rub ingredients in a small bowl and set aside. Combine the ingredients for the spritz in a spray bottle or bowl and set aside.

Cube the pork belly into 1-inch (2.5-cm) pieces and toss with the yellow mustard in a bowl until evenly coated. Season all over with the dry rub. Let sit at room temperature while your cooker comes up to temperature.

Preheat your cooker to 250°F (121°C). If you're using a kamado or bullet grill, add two or three chunks of smoking wood to the charcoal; with a pellet grill, simply preheat the cooker, as the pellets will take care of the smokey flavor. Once the cooker is ready, arrange your pork belly on a wire baking rack, then place the rack with the pork in the smoker. Let it cook for 1 hour.

At the 1-hour mark, check the cubes for an internal temperature of 190°F (88°C). If they have not reached 190°F (88°C), mop or spray the pork belly with the spritz mixture. Continue cooking and checking every 30 minutes until the correct temperature is reached, typically 1 to 2 hours. When the internal temperature measures 190°F (88°C), pull out the pork belly cubes. Place them in an aluminum pan and set aside.

To make the sauce, mix together the soy sauce, vinegar, cornstarch, sambal oelek, Shaoxing wine and sugar and set aside. In a medium saucepan, heat the peanut oil over medium heat and sauté the leeks, white parts of the scallions, garlic and ginger until fragrant, 1 to 2 minutes. Add the Chinese dry chile peppers and stir for 1 minute. Then mix in the soy sauce mixture. Bring to a low boil, reduce the heat to medium-low and simmer for 10 minutes.

Pour the sauce over the pork belly cubes in the aluminum pan, cover with foil and put back in the smoker for 30 to 60 minutes. After the first 30 minutes, check the progress by gently lifting a corner of the foil and checking for two things: Is the pork belly probe-tender and has the sauce set? If yes to both, you are done. If not, keep cooking and checking every 15 minutes.

When ready, pour the sauced pork belly in a serving bowl and toss with the Sichuan peppercorns, reserved scallion tops and peanuts.

GREEK-STYLE STUFFED PORK TENDERLOIN
WITH BALSAMIC GLAZE

The flavors you find in many Greek dishes complement pork very well. The balsamic glaze with the fresh rosemary really makes this dish special. If you are looking for a recipe that will be a great centerpiece for a dinner party, this is it!

FEEDS: 4–6

SUGGESTED WOOD: Apple, pecan or cherry chips

APPROXIMATE TOTAL COOK TIME: 1 hour, including making the glaze

GRILL SETUP: Direct

GREEK STUFFING
1 tsp olive oil

Pinch of red pepper flakes

3 cloves garlic, grated

3 cups (90 g) packed baby spinach

Pinch of kosher salt

2 oz (57 g) roasted red peppers, chopped

2 oz (57 g) Kalamata olives, chopped

2 oz (57 g) crumbled feta cheese

PORK TENDERLOIN
2 (1½-lb [680-g]) pork tenderloins

Salt and pepper

BALSAMIC GLAZE
1 cup (240 ml) balsamic vinegar

3 tbsp (42 g) light brown sugar, packed

2 medium cloves garlic, minced

2 tsp (1 g) fresh chopped rosemary

1 tsp salt

First, make the Greek stuffing. Heat the oil in a small skillet over medium heat. Add the red pepper flakes and garlic. Sauté until fragrant, about 30 seconds. Add the spinach and allow it to wilt, 2 to 3 minutes. Sprinkle lightly with salt, then remove the mixture from the heat. Let it sit at room temperature until it's cool enough to handle, about 10 minutes. Place the spinach mixture in a piece of cheesecloth and squeeze gently to release as much moisture as you can. Place the spinach in a bowl and stir in the chopped peppers, olives and feta cheese. Set aside.

Prep the tenderloins. Slice the tenderloins down the middle lengthwise. Open the tenderloins like you would a book and lay them flat. Place a piece of plastic wrap over the tenderloins and, using a meat mallet, pound the meat until it is ½ inch (1.3 cm) thick. Spread the stuffing mixture evenly down the center of the tenderloins, leaving ½ inch (1.3 cm) on the top and bottom without stuffing.

Roll up the outside of the long edge of the tenderloins like you would a newspaper, keeping the stuffing intact. Make sure to tuck in the ends as you roll to prevent the stuffing from coming out during the cook. Once you have rolled up the pork tenderloins, use butcher's twine to tie it together in four or five places. Season with kosher salt and freshly ground black pepper.

To make the glaze, mix the balsamic vinegar with the brown sugar, garlic, rosemary and salt in a saucepan over medium heat, stirring constantly until the sugar has dissolved, about 5 minutes. Bring the mixture to a low boil, reduce the heat to low and simmer until the glaze is reduced by half and is thick enough to coat the back of a spoon, about 30 minutes. Set aside to cool.

Preheat your cooker to 350°F (177°C). If you're using a kamado or bullet grill, add a handful of wood chips to the charcoal; with a pellet grill, simply preheat the cooker, as the pellets will take care of the smokey flavor. Cook the pork tenderloins for 15 minutes, then flip to the other side; do a temperature check at this point to make sure the tenderloins are cooking evenly. Cook another 15 minutes or until they measure 145°F (63°C) internally.

Pull out the tenderloins and rest them for 10 minutes before slicing into disks 1 inch (2.5 cm) thick and drizzling the balsamic glaze over the pieces to serve.

VIETNAMESE-STYLE PORK TENDERLOIN

I love the flavors you find in Vietnamese food. Ingredients such as mint, fish sauce and lime work surprisingly well with American BBQ. Marinating the pork tenderloin in this sauce tenderizes the meat and leaves a lasting impression from the rich flavor profile. Serve this with lettuce, tomatoes and cucumbers for a delicious meal.

FEEDS: 4–6
SUGGESTED WOOD: Apple, hickory or cherry chips
APPROXIMATE TOTAL COOK TIME: 40 minutes, plus overnight for marinating
GRILL SETUP: Direct

PORK
2 (1½-lb [680-g]) pork tenderloins

MARINADE
¼ cup (60 ml) fish sauce

¼ cup (60 ml) fresh lime juice

¼ cup (55 g) brown sugar

4 cloves garlic, peeled

2 jalapeño peppers, stemmed and roughly chopped

1 bunch cilantro, roughly chopped

1 bunch scallions, roughly chopped

½ cup (46 g) mint leaves, roughly chopped

Kosher salt and freshly ground black pepper, to taste

TO SERVE
Sliced cucumber

Lettuce

Tomato

Trim the tenderloins by removing any excess fat and the silver skin. To remove the silver skin, slide the tip of a very sharp paring knife between the silver skin and the flesh and carefully glide the knife along the meat, pulling away the silver skin at the same time. This way, all sides will get flavor from the marinade.

Combine the marinade ingredients in a blender or food processor and blend until it forms a smooth paste. Place the trimmed pork tenderloins in a large resealable bag, pour in the marinade and refrigerate overnight.

Preheat your cooker to 350°F (177°C). If you're using a kamado or bullet grill, add a handful of wood chips to the charcoal; with a pellet grill, simply preheat the cooker, as the pellets will take care of the smokey flavor.

Place the tenderloins in the cooker and grill for 20 minutes. Flip to the other side and do a temperature check to make sure the tenderloins are cooking evenly. Cook for another 20 minutes or until the pork reaches an internal temperature of 145°F (63°C).

Pull out the pork and let it rest for 10 minutes. Slice and serve with sliced cucumber, lettuce and tomato.

SMOKED BEER-BRAISED PORK BELLY

Pork belly is so versatile. I love cooking with it any chance I get, as the fat and full flavor from this meat is a great canvas for many dishes. Because it is smoked first to get that BBQ flavor then braised for tenderness, this pork belly is so good you will wish you had made twice as much. This can be refrigerated for a week, sliced, then pan-fried and served as needed.

FEEDS: 12–16

SUGGESTED WOOD: Apple, hickory or cherry chunks

APPROXIMATE TOTAL COOK TIME: 4–5 hours

GRILL SETUP: Indirect

SPRITZ

½ cup (120 ml) apple juice

½ cup (120 ml) cider vinegar

PORK BELLY

1 (4-lb [1.8-kg]) slab pork belly (uncured)

1 tbsp (15 ml) yellow mustard

¼ cup (73 g) your favorite sweet and savory pork rub (I use Dizzy Pig Dizzy Dust)

12 oz (355 ml) your favorite beer (I love using a nice lager)

½ cup (120 ml) your favorite BBQ Sauce (my Cherry Coke BBQ Sauce on page 90 would be great here)

Combine the ingredients for the spritz in a spray bottle, or in a bowl if you plan to mop. Set it aside.

Preheat your cooker to 250°F (121°C). If you're using a kamado or bullet grill, add two or three chunks of smoking wood to the charcoal; with a pellet grill, simply preheat the cooker, as the pellets will take care of the smokey flavor.

Crosshatch-cut the top layer of fat on the pork belly by making a diagonal-cut pattern across the length of the meat. First space the scores evenly 1 inch (2.5 cm) apart to ensure proper cooking and presentation. Then turn the meat 90 degrees to add a crosshatch to each of the previous scores. Make sure to score only the fat and not cut into the meat. Apply a small amount of yellow mustard and spread it evenly across the entire surface of the pork belly. Generously apply the rub to all sides of the pork belly.

Place the pork belly in your cooker and smoke until the internal temperature reaches 165°F (74°C), 2½ to 3 hours, maintaining the cooker's temperature at 250°F (121°C). After the first hour, spritz or mop the surface of the pork belly every 30 minutes until you reach the next step. Make sure you focus on the fundamentals I have taught you to know when and where to add moisture to the meat cooking.

Once the pork belly reaches 165°F (74°C), remove it from the cooker and place it in a deep aluminum pan just big enough to fit the meat. Fill the bottom of the pan with the beer and tightly seal the opening with foil. Now place the pan into your smoker and cook until the internal temperature reaches 200°F (93°C). This will take 1 to 2 hours more. Check the internal temperature every 30 minutes, being careful when opening the foil, as steam will escape and can burn.

Once the pork reaches 200°F (93°C) internally, remove it from the foil and place on a cutting board. You can mop some of the pan drippings on the pork belly. Bump up the temperature of the cooker to 300°F (149°C). (For charcoal grillers, see page 34 for tips on adjusting the temperature. For pellet grillers, simply change the temperature.) Meanwhile, coat the top of the pork belly with the BBQ sauce. When the temperature is at 300°F (149°C), return the pork belly to the cooker for 10 to 20 minutes, until the sauce sets.

Remove the finished pork belly to a cutting board and let it rest for 10 to 20 minutes before slicing and serving.

BOLOGNA BURNT ENDS

WITH KIMCHI SLAW

This was the first recipe I thought of when tasked with writing this book. I was chatting with a good friend about how much fun it will be coming up with new recipes and as we started to bounce ideas off one another, this recipe was born. Now, remember the bologna is precooked, so you are just getting color and flavor into the meat. Have fun with this one . . . I know I did!

FEEDS: 10–12

SUGGESTED WOOD: Apple, hickory or cherry chunks

APPROXIMATE TOTAL COOK TIME: 3½ hours

GRILL SETUP: Indirect

KIMCHI SLAW

½ cup (120 ml) mayo

½ cup (120 ml) gochujang

2 tbsp (30 ml) seasoned rice vinegar

1 tsp fresh grated ginger root

1 clove garlic, grated

1 tsp honey

1 tbsp (15 ml) toasted sesame oil

½ head small Napa cabbage

3 scallions, white and green parts chopped

1 (6-inch [15-cm]) piece daikon radish, peeled, cut into matchsticks

2 cups (220 g) store-bought shredded carrots

½ cup (36 g) prepared kimchi, drained (1 tbsp [15 ml] sauce reserved)

BOLOGNA

3 lbs (1.4 kg) whole bologna chub

¼ cup (60 ml) yellow mustard

¼ cup (73 g) your favorite sweet and savory pork rub (I use Dizzy Pig Dizzy Dust)

½ cup (120 ml) BBQ sauce (the Gochujang Glaze from page 98 would be great here)

¼ cup (55 g) brown sugar

4 tbsp (57 g) butter, cut into ¼-inch (6-mm) cubes

TO SERVE

Toasted sesame seeds

Cilantro with tender stems

For the kimchi slaw, in a mixing bowl, whisk together the mayo, gochujang, rice vinegar, ginger, garlic and honey. Whisk in the sesame oil. Shred or chop the Napa cabbage and add that to the mixing bowl along with the scallions, daikon radish, carrots and kimchi. Then toss to coat the slaw in the dressing. Place in the fridge for the flavors to meld while you smoke the bologna.

Preheat your cooker to 225°F (107°C). If you're using a kamado or bullet grill, add two or three chunks of smoking wood to the charcoal; with a pellet grill, simply preheat the cooker, as the pellets will take care of the smokey flavor. Using a sharp knife, slightly score the bologna (about ¼ inch [6 mm] deep) in a crosshatch pattern on all sides. Slather the chub with the yellow mustard and then cover all sides with the BBQ rub, making sure to work the rub into the crosshatch cuts you just made. Place the bologna in the cooker and smoke it undisturbed for 3 hours, maintaining the temperature at 225°F (107°C).

After 3 hours, take the smoked chub off the cooker and dice it into 1½-inch (4-cm) cubes. Place the cubes into an aluminum pan and toss with the BBQ sauce, then top with the sugar and butter. Bump up the temperature of your cooker to 250°F (121°C). For charcoal grillers, do this by opening the vents to match the grilling setup of your cooker outlined on page 34 in Fundamental 3: Controlling Temperature and the BBQ Zone. For pellet grillers, simply set the new temperature. When the temperature is stable, place the bologna cubes in and cook for another 30 minutes to an hour, until the sauce sets.

Remove the bologna burnt ends, place them in a bowl and serve with kimchi slaw on the side or over the bologna. Garnish with sesame seeds and cilantro.

PINEAPPLE-CHIPOTLE GLAZED BONE-IN RACK OF PORK

This is one of my favorite recipes to serve during the holidays. A bone-in rack of pork is not only delicious but makes a great centerpiece for the table. This cut is essentially a pork loin with the rib bones intact, giving you several options to cook and present to guests. From slicing it into double-cut pork chops or forming a pork crown roast, this is one of my favorite pork cuts to work with. Talk to your local butcher about getting this cut of pork, or order it online from Snake River Farms, which is where I get mine. The balance between sweet and heat in this glaze is perfect. You can dial up the spiciness by adding one or more chipotle peppers to the glaze.

FEEDS: 10

SUGGESTED WOOD: Apple, pecan or hickory chunks

APPROXIMATE TOTAL COOK TIME: 1½ hours

GRILL SETUP: Indirect

GLAZE

1 (7-oz [199-g]) can chipotle peppers in adobo sauce

1 pineapple, cored and diced

1 cup (240 ml) honey

½ cup (120 ml) apple cider vinegar

¼ tsp ground nutmeg

½ tsp kosher salt

PORK

1 (6-lb [3-kg]) bone-in rack of pork

1 tbsp (15 ml) yellow mustard

1 tbsp (18 g) your favorite sweet and savory pork rub (I use Dizzy Pig Raging River)

For the glaze, remove the chipotles from the adobo sauce and discard, saving the adobo sauce for the glaze. Or if you want the glaze to be spicier, you can add one or more of the chipotle peppers to the glaze as well—I add two peppers to my glaze. Combine the adobo sauce (and peppers, if you're using them), diced pineapple, honey, cider vinegar, ground nutmeg and salt in a blender. Blend thoroughly. If the mix is too thick, add 1 to 3 tablespoons (15 to 45 ml) of water. Pour the mixture into a saucepan and bring it to a boil, then reduce the heat to low. Cook for 15 minutes, until the glaze thickens and coats the back of a spoon.

Preheat the cooker to 325°F (163°C). If you're using a kamado or bullet grill, add two or three chunks of smoking wood to the charcoal; with a pellet grill, simply preheat the cooker, as the pellets will take care of the smokey flavor. While the cooker is coming up to temperature, take the rack of pork out of the packaging and apply the yellow mustard evenly on all sides of the meat. Next, cover the rack of pork with the rub on all sides and let it come to room temperature before adding to your cooker.

Add the rack of pork to the cooker and let it cook undisturbed for 1 hour before checking the temperature. At this point the internal temperature should be around 125°F (52°C). Now, brush the glaze all over the rack of pork, reserving the remainder of the glaze for serving. Let the pork cook another 10 to 20 minutes, until the internal temperature is 145°F (63°C).

Remove the pork and let it rest for 10 minutes. Serve with the remaining glaze.

THINGS THAT GO "CLUCK" (. . . AND "GOBBLE")

We cannot forget about our fine feathered friends! In this chapter, you will find chicken recipes that are so delicious you will make them again and again. From whole chicken recipes to chicken wings and everything in between, you will learn techniques to make any poultry dish sing! In this chapter, you will learn how to spatchcock a chicken, how to use a dry brine for crispy skin and much more. The fundamentals learned at the start of this book will help you get that smokey flavor in any chicken dish.

SMOKED SPATCHCOCK CHICKEN

WITH SPICY ALABAMA WHITE SAUCE

Smoked chicken is one of my favorite comfort foods. If I am not careful, I could eat an entire chicken as it comes off the cooker. I did my own spin on Alabama white sauce by adding gochujaru and sriracha for added kick. You won't be able to stop dunking the chicken in the sauce once you get started.

FEEDS: 2–4
SUGGESTED WOOD: Oak, hickory or apple chips
APPROXIMATE TOTAL COOK TIME: 2–2½ hours
GRILL SETUP: Indirect

SPICY ALABAMA WHITE SAUCE

1 cup (240 ml) mayonnaise

¼ cup (60 ml) apple cider vinegar

2 tbsp (30 ml) sriracha

1 tsp Worcestershire sauce

1 tsp lemon juice

2 tbsp (30 g) sugar

½ tsp garlic powder

½ tsp onion powder

¼ tsp gochujaru pepper (or red pepper flakes)

SPATCHCOCK CHICKEN

1 (4–5-lb [1.8–2.5-kg]) whole chicken

1 tbsp (15 ml) olive oil

¼ cup (73 g) your favorite seasoning (I use Dizzy Pig Wonder Bird)

For the sauce, mix all the sauce ingredients together in a bowl, pour all but ½ cup (120 ml) into a container and set aside. Reserve the ½ cup (120 ml) of sauce for dipping the chicken when serving.

Take the chicken out of the packaging and pat it dry with paper towels. Next, place the chicken on a cutting board with the legs pointing toward you, breast side down. Use kitchen shears to cut along the backbone on both sides; remove the backbone. (Note: You can reserve the backbone to make stock later if you want to.) Flip over the chicken so the breast side is facing up toward you. Use your hands to press down firmly, breaking the sternum and flattening the chicken like an open book. Rub the chicken all over with the olive oil for a base and apply the seasoning evenly.

Preheat your cooker to 250°F (121°C). If you're using a kamado or bullet grill, add a handful of wood chips to the charcoal; with a pellet grill, simply preheat the cooker, as the pellets will take care of the smokey flavor. When the cooker is ready, place the chicken in breast side up. Let the chicken cook for 1 hour or until the breast reaches an internal temperature of 150°F (66°C).

At this point, take out the chicken, place in an aluminum pan, glaze the chicken generously with the spicy white sauce and put the chicken in the pan back in the cooker until the breast measures 165°F (73°C) internally. This could take 1 to 1½ hours before reaching the desired temperature.

Remove the chicken and let it rest for 10 minutes. Carve and serve with the reserved white sauce.

CILANTRO AND LIME CHICKEN HALVES

Cilantro and lime are the perfect ingredients to marinate chicken. Marry those flavors with garlic and jalapeño and you have an amazing chicken dish for two! Serving the charred chicken with extra lime and cilantro as garnish makes for a beautiful dinner presentation.

FEEDS: 2–4

SUGGESTED WOOD: Pecan, hickory or apple chips

APPROXIMATE TOTAL COOK TIME: 1½ hours

GRILL SETUP: Indirect

1 (4–5-lb [1.8–2.5-kg]) whole chicken

1 bunch of cilantro, roughly chopped

4 cloves garlic, roughly chopped

3 jalapeños, seeded, roughly chopped

¼ cup (60 ml) olive oil

3 limes, juiced

1 tsp cumin

1 tsp salt

1 tsp black pepper

Take the chicken out of the packaging and pat it dry with paper towels. Next, place the chicken on a cutting board with the legs pointing toward you, breast side down. Use kitchen shears to cut along the backbone on both sides; remove the backbone. (Note: You can reserve the backbone to make stock later if you want to.) Flip over the chicken so the breast side is facing up and slice down the center of the chicken, dividing it in two equal halves. Place the chicken halves in a large resealable bag and set aside.

To make the marinade, combine the cilantro, garlic, jalapeños, olive oil, lime juice, cumin, salt and pepper in food processor or blender and blend until it forms a thick paste. Pour the marinade over the chicken halves in the bag and refrigerate overnight.

Preheat the cooker to 350°F (177°C). If you're using a kamado or bullet grill, add a handful of wood chips to the charcoal; with a pellet grill, simply preheat the cooker, as the pellets will take care of the smokey flavor. Take the chicken out of the marinade and let it come to room temp while the cooker preheats. Once the cooker is ready, place the chicken inside and cook until it measures 165°F (74°C) using an instant-read meat thermometer in the breast, about 1½ hours.

Remove the chicken and let it rest for 10 minutes before serving.

SWEET AND SOUR CHICKEN WINGS

I love chicken wings any way they come. The crispy skin, smokey flavor and saucy deliciousness gets me every time. This glaze is well balanced between sweet and sour and goes so well with chicken wings. When the wings are glazed, the presentation is beautiful and will feed you with your eyes first. You will wish you had more of these when they're gone.

FEEDS: 4–6 as an appetizer

SUGGESTED WOOD: Apple, hickory or pecan chips

APPROXIMATE TOTAL COOK TIME: 40 minutes

GRILL SETUP: Indirect

GLAZE

¼ cup (60 ml) pineapple juice

1 tbsp (8 g) cornstarch

¼ cup (60 ml) rice vinegar

¼ cup (55 g) brown sugar

¼ cup (60 ml) ketchup

1 tbsp (15 ml) soy sauce

1 tbsp (15 ml) honey

1 tsp sriracha

CHICKEN

2 lbs (907 g) chicken wings

2 tsp (12 g) your favorite savory poultry rub (I use Dizzy Pig Peking seasoning)

Sliced scallions, for garnish

In a small bowl, mix together the pineapple juice and cornstarch until a smooth slurry is formed. This is important to help thicken the sauce for the wings. Next whisk together the rice vinegar, brown sugar, ketchup, soy sauce, honey, sriracha and the slurry in a saucepan. Heat the mixture over medium heat, stirring often, until the sauce thickens, about 15 minutes. Set aside while you cook the chicken wings.

Preheat the cooker to 350°F (176°C). If you're using a kamado or bullet grill, add a handful of wood chips to the charcoal; with a pellet grill, simply preheat the cooker, as the pellets will take care of the smokey flavor. Rub the chicken wings evenly with the rub. Cook the wings for 20 minutes. Flip and cook for another 20 minutes or until the internal temperature is 165°F (74°C).

Remove the wings and place them in a large bowl. Pour the glaze over the top of the chicken wings and toss until evenly coated. Garnish with scallions, serve and enjoy!

HABANERO AND MANGO-GLAZED CHICKEN WINGS

This chicken wing recipe reminds me of visiting the Caribbean and sitting outside at a beach café, eating and drinking after a morning beach visit. The glaze for the wings finds the right balance between sweet and spicy. This is a great dish for your main meal or to get your party started.

FEEDS: 4–6 as an appetizer

SUGGESTED WOOD: Apple or pecan chips

APPROXIMATE TOTAL COOK TIME: 50 minutes

GRILL SETUP: Indirect

GLAZE

2 large, ripe mangoes, diced

1 habanero pepper, deseeded, deveined and minced

¼ cup (60 ml) honey

½ cup (120 ml) apple cider vinegar

1 tbsp (15 ml) soy sauce

1 tbsp (15 ml) lime juice

¾ cup (180 ml) water

CHICKEN WINGS

2 lbs (907 g) chicken wings

1 tbsp (15 ml) olive oil

Pinch of kosher salt and black pepper

To make the glaze, add all the glaze ingredients in a saucepan, stir to incorporate and cook over medium-low for 15 minutes until the mangoes are soft. Pour into a blender or food processor to mix until you form a smooth paste. Set aside.

Preheat the cooker to 350°F (177°C). If you're using a kamado or bullet grill, add a handful of wood chips to the charcoal; with a pellet grill, simply preheat the cooker, as the pellets will take care of the smokey flavor. Take the wings out of the fridge, letting them come up to room temperature while the cooker heats up. Toss the wings with the olive oil, salt and pepper in a large bowl. (Note: For a different flavor profile, you can use your favorite BBQ rub.)

Place the wings on the cooker and let them cook for 20 minutes. Flip and let the wings cook for another 20 minutes, or until they are deep brown and reach an internal temperature of 165°F (74°C).

Remove the wings, place them in a large bowl and toss them with the glaze. Place the glazed wings back into the cooker for 10 minutes, until the sauce sets. Serve the wings with extra glaze for dipping.

THAI GREEN CURRY CHICKEN WINGS

Green curry is so pungent and delicious it makes a perfect marinade for chicken. The coconut milk helps tenderize the chicken wings and marry all of these wonderful flavors together. You can serve this with fresh lime and extra cilantro for added flavor.

FEEDS: 4–6 as an appetizer
SUGGESTED WOOD: Apple, hickory or pecan chips
APPROXIMATE TOTAL COOK TIME: 40 minutes, plus overnight for marinating
GRILL SETUP: Indirect

MARINADE

1 tbsp (15 ml) green curry paste

6 cloves garlic, minced

1 tbsp (15 g) sugar

½ cup (120 ml) coconut milk

2 tbsp (30 ml) soy sauce

2 tbsp (30 ml) fish sauce

1 (1-inch [2.5-cm]) piece of fresh ginger, grated

½ a bunch of cilantro, minced, plus more for garnish

CHICKEN

2 lbs (907 g) chicken wings

Lime wedges, for serving

In a food processor or blender, combine the curry paste, garlic, sugar, coconut milk, soy sauce, fish sauce, ginger and cilantro. Blend into a smooth sauce. Place the chicken wings in a large resealable bag and then add the marinade. Place the bag in the refrigerator and marinate for 8 hours or overnight, turning the bag at least once midway through.

Remove the chicken from the marinade and preheat your cooker to 350°F (177°C). If you're using a kamado or bullet grill, add a handful of wood chips to the charcoal; with a pellet grill, simply preheat the cooker, as the pellets will take care of the smokey flavor. Add the chicken wings to the cooker and let them cook for 20 minutes. Flip and cook for 20 minutes more, or until the chicken measures 165°F (74°C) internally.

Remove the chicken wings, garnish with fresh cilantro and serve with lime wedges.

BOURBON AND DIJON-GLAZED CHICKEN DRUMSTICKS

Chicken drumsticks do not get as much attention as other parts of the chicken. I hope this recipe changes that for you as it did for me. This bourbon and Dijon mustard glaze pairs nicely with the grilled chicken. You will want to be careful eating these, as your glazed fingers may be in play!

FEEDS: 6
SUGGESTED WOOD: Apple or pecan chips
APPROXIMATE TOTAL COOK TIME: 40–60 minutes
GRILL SETUP: Indirect

DRY RUB
1 tbsp (8 g) kosher salt
1 tbsp (6 g) black pepper
1 tsp paprika
1 tsp mustard powder
1 tsp garlic powder

CHICKEN
1 tbsp (15 ml) yellow mustard
12 chicken drumsticks (about 3 lbs [1.4 kg])

BOURBON AND DIJON GLAZE
3 tbsp (45 ml) Dijon mustard
2 oz (59 ml) bourbon
½ cup (120 ml) honey
1 tsp sriracha sauce
1 tbsp (15 ml) soy sauce

Preheat your cooker to 300°F (149°C). If you're using a kamado or bullet grill, add a handful of wood chips to the charcoal; with a pellet grill, simply preheat the cooker, as the pellets will take care of the smokey flavor.

Mix the salt, pepper, paprika, mustard powder and garlic powder together in a small bowl. Slather yellow mustard lightly on each drumstick. Cover the drumsticks with the dry rub evenly on all sides. Add the drumsticks to the cooker and let them cook until the internal temperature reaches 180°F (82°C), about 40 minutes. I like to flip the drumsticks after 20 minutes in to ensure even color all around.

For the glaze, mix the mustard, bourbon, honey, sriracha and soy sauce in a saucepan and heat over medium heat, stirring frequently. After the mixture comes to a boil, reduce and simmer for about 20 minutes or until the sauce thickens; ideally it will coat the back of a spoon.

Remove the chicken from your cooker and dip each drumstick in the glaze, coating them evenly. Place the glazed drumsticks back into your cooker and cook to let the sauce set, about 10 minutes.

Pull off the drumsticks and let them rest for 10 minutes before serving.

TANGY FILIPINO CHICKEN DRUMSTICKS

I love the flavors of Filipino food: sour, garlicky, salty and most of all comforting. This recipe balances those flavors with some lemon-lime soda for sweetness and tenderness. The texture and taste of the chicken skin is second to none. Served in a big bowl with scallion garnish, this dish makes a beautiful presentation when hitting the table.

FEEDS: 6

SUGGESTED WOOD: Apple, pecan or hickory chips

APPROXIMATE TOTAL COOK TIME: 45–55 minutes, plus overnight for marinating

GRILL SETUP: Indirect

MARINADE

¾ cup (180 ml) white vinegar

¾ cup (180 ml) lemon-lime soda

½ cup (120 ml) soy sauce

½ cup (120 ml) ketchup

¼ cup (60 ml) lime juice

6 cloves garlic, minced

1 tsp salt

1 tsp black pepper

½ tsp cayenne pepper

CHICKEN

3 lbs (1.4 kg) chicken drumsticks

Chopped scallion, for garnish

In a large bowl, combine all the ingredients for the marinade. Put the chicken and the marinade in a large resealable bag. Place the bag in the refrigerator and marinate for 8 hours or overnight.

Preheat your cooker to 350°F (177°C). If you're using a kamado or bullet grill, add a handful of wood chips to the charcoal; with a pellet grill, simply preheat the cooker, as the pellets will take care of the smokey flavor.

Once the cooker is up to temperature, remove the chicken from the marinade and place it inside. Let the drumsticks cook for 35 minutes, turning occasionally to cook the chicken evenly on all sides. You will see a deep mahogany color form on the chicken skin.

Check the internal temperature, and when it measures 175°F (79°C) (this could take an additional 10 to 20 minutes), pull out the chicken and let it rest for 10 minutes before serving with the chopped scallion.

CUBANO STUFFED CHICKEN BREASTS

One of my favorite sandwiches is a pressed Cuban sandwich. The pork, ham, cheese and pickle combination work so well. For this recipe, my goal was to find out if stuffing a chicken breast with ham, cheese and pickles, then wrapping it in bacon would produce a similar experience. I was right and this dish is a winning combination.

FEEDS: 4
SUGGESTED WOOD: Apple, pecan or mesquite chips
APPROXIMATE TOTAL COOK TIME: 40 minutes–1 hour
GRILL SETUP: Indirect

---

4 medium-sized chicken breasts

2 tbsp (30 ml) Dijon mustard

4 slices Swiss cheese, cut into quarters

4 slices thinly sliced deli ham, cut into quarters

12 dill pickle chips

8 thickly sliced pieces of bacon

Butterfly the chicken breasts by placing your hand on top of one and then slicing horizontally into one side. Start at the thicker end and finish at the thinner end, without slicing through to the other side. Open the chicken breast and notice the butterfly shape (thus the name). Cover with plastic wrap and use a meat tenderizer to pound the chicken flat; it should be no more than ½ inch (1.3 cm) thick. Spread mustard evenly over one side of the flattened chicken breasts. Repeat with the remaining breasts.

Now place 1 slice (4 quarters) each of Swiss cheese and ham on each breast. Place 3 pickles on top of the ham, down the middle of the chicken breast.

Roll up the chicken breast, sealing the ingredients inside. Wrap a piece of bacon around the middle of the chicken breast widthwise, then another one lengthwise, sealing the contents inside with bacon. Secure the bacon using toothpicks; make sure to place one through the bottom of the chicken breast to help keep the contents inside while cooking.

Preheat your smoker to 350°F (177°C). If you're using a kamado or bullet grill, add a handful of wood chips to the charcoal; with a pellet grill, simply preheat the cooker, as the pellets will take care of the smokey flavor. When the smoker is ready, put the chicken in and let cook for 20 minutes, then flip and cook for another 20 minutes before checking the internal temperature. If the chicken breasts measure 165°F (74°C), they are ready. If not, cook for another 20 minutes and check again. When ready, pull the chicken off the grill and let it rest for 10 minutes before slicing and serving.

FRESH CHIMICHURRI CHICKEN SKEWERS

I love the bright, vibrant flavor of fresh chimichurri. I have always added this sauce to steaks and never thought about pairing it with chicken. This recipe was born when I had some reserved chimichurri on hand and wanted to make an easy chicken appetizer for some guests. The richness of the chicken thighs matches the acidity of the chimichurri so well.

FEEDS: 4–6 as an appetizer

SUGGESTED WOOD: Pecan, oak or hickory chips

APPROXIMATE TOTAL COOK TIME: 40–60 minutes, plus 2 to 3 hours for marinating

GRILL SETUP: Indirect

CHIMICHURRI SAUCE
2 cups (32 g) finely chopped fresh cilantro

1 cup (60 g) finely chopped fresh parsley

4 cloves garlic, minced

2 tsp (5 g) red chili flakes

1 jalapeño, seeded and minced

½ cup (120 ml) olive oil

½ cup (120 ml) red wine vinegar

Kosher salt, to taste

CHICKEN
2 lbs (907 g) boneless, skinless chicken thighs

GARNISH
Cilantro

Jalapeño slices

Lime wedges

In a large bowl, mix the cilantro, parsley, garlic, chili flakes, jalapeño, olive oil and red wine vinegar until well combined; add salt to taste. Reserve some of the chimichurri sauce for serving later and pour the rest into a large resealable bag.

Trim the fat from the chicken thighs and cube them into 1-inch (2.5-cm) pieces. Add the cubed chicken to the sauce in the bag and refrigerate for 2 to 3 hours to marinate. While the chicken is marinating, soak wooden skewers in water, at least 1 hour.

Preheat your cooker to 350°F (177°C). If you're using a kamado or bullet grill, add a handful of wood chips to the charcoal; with a pellet grill, simply preheat the cooker, as the pellets will take care of the smokey flavor. Skewer the marinated chicken pieces on the soaked wooden skewers, four or five pieces per skewer. The chicken will cook more evenly if you avoid crowding the chicken pieces on the skewers.

Cook the chicken skewers for 20 minutes, then flip to get an equal amount of color on all sides. Cook for another 20 minutes, then check the internal temperature of the chicken. When the internal temperature reaches 165°F (74°C), pull the skewers from the cooker and let them rest for 10 minutes.

Garnish with the reserved chimichurri sauce, cilantro and jalapeño. Serve with fresh lime slices for an extra pop of citrus flavor.

SPICY ASIAN CHICKEN MEATBALLS

As you may have noticed, I am heavily influenced by Asian flavors. This dish was inspired from a local Thai restaurant and their amazing chicken satay. I wanted to do something that could easily be made ahead of time and cooked on your smoker when you are close to mealtime. This can be the perfect appetizer for your next gathering.

FEEDS: 4 as an appetizer

SUGGESTED WOOD: Apple, hickory or pecan chips

APPROXIMATE TOTAL COOK TIME: 30–40 minutes

GRILL SETUP: Indirect

PEANUT SAUCE

1 tbsp (15 ml) vegetable oil

2 tbsp (20 g) chopped red onion

1 tsp chili powder

¼ cup (60 ml) coconut milk

2 tbsp (32 g) creamy peanut butter

2 tbsp (30 ml) hot water

1 tbsp (15 ml) fresh lime juice

3 tbsp (27 g) chopped salted peanuts, divided

Kosher salt, to taste

CHICKEN MEATBALLS

1 lb (454 g) ground chicken

¼ cup (40 g) finely chopped red onion

1 egg

½ cup (28 g) panko breadcrumbs

1 tbsp (15 ml) olive oil

1 tsp chili powder

1 tsp kosher salt

1 tsp garam masala

Vegetable oil, for brushing the meatballs

Make the peanut sauce by heating the vegetable oil over medium heat in a saucepan. Add the chopped onion and chili powder. Cook over medium heat, stirring, until the onion is softened, about 5 minutes. Add the coconut milk and bring to a low boil. Remove from the heat and whisk in the peanut butter, hot water and lime juice. Stir in 2 tablespoons (18 g) peanuts and season the sauce lightly with salt. Set aside while the meatballs are cooking.

For the chicken meatballs, combine the ground chicken with the chopped onion, egg, panko breadcrumbs, olive oil, chili powder, salt and garam masala and mix together evenly. Form the ground chicken mixture into nine (2-ounce [57-g]) meatballs. A kitchen scale is helpful to get the meatballs all the same size.

Preheat the cooker to 350°F (177°C). If you're using a kamado or bullet grill, add a handful of wood chips to the charcoal; with a pellet grill, simply preheat the cooker, as the pellets will take care of the smokey flavor.

Place the meatballs on a wire baking rack and brush them with vegetable oil. Put the wire rack with the oiled meatballs in the grill. Cook for 15 minutes, then flip over the meatballs so all sides get even coloring. Cook for another 15 to 20 minutes, or until the meatballs measure 165°F (74°C) internally.

When done, remove the meatballs and let them cool slightly before drizzling some of the peanut sauce on top and sprinkling on the remaining peanuts. The remaining sauce can be used for dipping.

JAMAICAN JERK SMOKED TURKEY BREAST

My wife and I got married in Jamaica and visit there every year on our anniversary. When there, I eat as much authentic jerk cooking as I can. I had to include at least one recipe using my version of the classic jerk marinade. This marinade will work well on chicken and pork, too.

FEEDS: 10–12
SUGGESTED WOOD: Allspice berries and bay leaves (see directions)
APPROXIMATE TOTAL COOK TIME: 3–4 hours, plus overnight for marinating
GRILL SETUP: Indirect

JERK MARINADE

1 tbsp (6 g) allspice berries, divided

24 dried bay leaves, divided

1 tbsp (6 g) whole black peppercorns

4 to 6 whole Scotch bonnet peppers, stems removed

6 scallions, white and green parts roughly chopped

1 large shallot, peeled

1 (2-inch [5-cm]) piece ginger, roughly chopped

6 large cloves garlic, smashed

3 tbsp (45 g) brown sugar

2 tbsp (4 g) fresh thyme leaves

2 tbsp (5 g) finely grated lime zest

2 tbsp (60 ml) fresh lime juice

2 tbsp (60 ml) canola oil

½ tsp freshly grated nutmeg

2 tsp (6 g) kosher salt

TURKEY

1 (3–4-lb [1.4–1.8-kg]) skin-on, deboned turkey breast

1 cup (227 g) butter, softened at room temperature

Sliced scallions, for garnish

In a large bowl, mix together ½ tablespoon (3 g) of allspice berries, 12 bay leaves and the rest of the marinade ingredients. Remove the skin from the turkey breast and cover with the marinade in a sealed container. Place the container in the fridge overnight to marinate. The next day, remove the turkey from the marinade while you set up the cooker; discard the marinade.

If you are using either a kamado or bullet grill, about an hour before cooking the turkey breast take the remaining ½ tablespoon (3 g) of the allspice berries and 12 bay leaves and place them in a bowl of water to soak while you get your cooker up to temperature (see Note). Preheat the cooker to 250°F (121°C). Kamado or bullet grillers, add the soaked allspice berries and bay leaves to the lit charcoal right before adding the turkey to the cooker.

> ## ★ NOTE ★
>
> Traditional jerk is made using pimento wood but that is hard to get in the United States. Allspice berries come from the same tree and can be used to create smoke similar to that of pimento wood. In addition, I added some bay leaves to the lighted charcoal to get that jerk smoke flavor during my cook. If you are cooking this recipe on a pellet grill, skip this step as there are no live coals to which to add the aromatics. (I have seen pimento wood pellets for sale online if you want to go the extra step here.)

Put the turkey in the cooker placing the breast side (where you removed the skin) facing up and cook for 2½ hours, then remove the turkey. Cover the breast in butter, then double wrap it in foil to seal. Place the wrapped turkey back in the cooker, placing the breast side (where you removed the skin) down this time, and cook until the internal temperature reaches 165°F (74°C). This could take 30 minutes to an hour.

Remove the turkey breast from the cooker, crack the foil and let the turkey rest until the internal temperature drops to 140°F (60°C), about 20 minutes. Slice, garnish with the scallions and serve.

ACKNOWLEDGMENTS

To my wife, best friend and partner, Debbie Sussman (a.k.a. "Mrs. Buddha"). This book would not have happened if it were not for you. Your tireless support, planning and patience are more than I deserve. Thank you from the bottom of my heart.

To my children, Jessica and Zachary. I couldn't be prouder of the two of you and the adults you have grown to be. Your constant support for me while making the transition from IT executive to pit master will never be forgotten.

To the Buckman family: John, Judy, Michael, Julie, Madeline and Carter. Describing you as "in-laws" just doesn't convey who you are to me. Your constant support and encouragement mean more than you know.

Thank you to Snake River Farms for sponsoring me and for sending me all the delicious meat to use for this book. You make me feel like an extended part of the family.

Thank you to Bob, Jodi and Rob at Big Green Egg for giving me the opportunities you have and for your constant support.

Thank you to Traeger and Weber Grills. Your support and guidance as I put this book together was timely and helpful.

Thank you to Sara Rounsavall. You are an amazing food stylist and made the process of taking photographs for this book joyful.

Thank you to Sarah, Will and the entire team at Page Street Publishing for making this process easy and enjoyable.

Thanks to all of you who follow and support me. I hope I give back a small slice of what I get from you every day.

ABOUT THE AUTHOR

Chris Sussman

CHRIS SUSSMAN, a.k.a. The BBQ Buddha, has been a backyard pit master since 2009. He first started honing his craft in the Washington, DC, area, before making the move to Louisville, Kentucky, in 2017. Chris is a member of the Big Green Egg Pro Team and can be seen on their website and social media channels.

In October 2018, Chris decided he was ready to turn The BBQ Buddha into his full-time gig. He relaunched the brand and website and expanded his offerings to include catering services and grilling classes. Since that time Chris's Instagram account, @the_bbq_buddha, has more than quadrupled in audience following, visited by more than 600,000 visitors annually.

Chris has also been featured in major online publications such as Maxim, Thrillist and HuffPost. Chris has worked with major national brands such as Ace Hardware, Budweiser, Sierra Nevada Brewing, Walmart and many others.

INDEX